Check Your
COMMITMENT

Studies from Matthew

REFERENCE
226.206
Sta

Restoration

Staton, Knofel

Check Your
Commitment

by Knofel Staton

STANDARD PUBLISHING

Cincinnati, Ohio   39983

FLORIDA
CHRISTIAN
COLLEGE
LIBRARY

Unless otherwise indicated, all Scriptures are from the New American Standard Bible, © 1960, 1962, 1963, 1968, 1971, 1972, 1973, 1975, 1977 by the Lockman Foundation. Used by permission.

Sharing the thoughts of his own heart, the author may express views that are not entirely consistent with those of the publisher.

Library of Congress Cataloging in Publication Data

Staton, Knofel.
　Check your commitment.

　　1. Bible　N.T.　Matthew—Meditations.　2. Commitment to the church.
3. Christian life—Biblical teaching.
I. Title.
BS2575.4.S8 1985　　226'.206　　84-8819
ISBN 0-87239-829-3
ISBN 0-87239-828-5 (leader's ed.)

Copyright © 1985. The STANDARD PUBLISHING Company, Cincinnati, Ohio.
A division of STANDEX INTERNATIONAL Corporation. Printed in U.S.A.

DEDICATION

This book is appreciatively dedicated to two people who have been in the midst of the waves and yet "walk on water": Loretta and Beth

IN APPRECIATION

I continually feel a bit of sorrow, but at the same time appreciation beyond words, for anyone who has to read my handwriting. But to type an entire book from it—well! Thanks to Loretta Jane Buchanan, a person with a secretary's hand and head and a servant's heart.

Knofel Staton

TABLE OF CONTENTS

by Knofel Staton

God's List: Then and Now

(Matthew 1:1-17)

He came in history, but existed before time began. He was born, but was never begotten by man.

That's Jesus!

Messiah for the Jews

Matthew began his Gospel with the words, "The book of the genealogy of Jesus Christ, the son of David, the son of Abraham."

The word "genealogy" means "record of beginning." However, Matthew did not intend for us to see that Jesus' origin went no farther back than Abraham. Matthew was with Jesus when He said to the Jews, "Truly, truly, I say to you, before Abraham was born, I am" (John 8:58).

Just how far back does Jesus go? "He was in the beginning with God" (John 1:2). Then why did Matthew trace Jesus' genealogy back to Abraham and no farther? Matthew wrote the genealogy of Jesus with a purpose. He wanted the Jews to know that Jesus was the Messiah that God promised would come through the family tree of Abraham.

From that first sentence, Matthew systematically pulled away the props that some Jews were using to support their reasons for not accepting the Messiahship of Jesus. Matthew made it clear that Jesus fulfilled Jewish prophecy about the Messiah.

Jesus fulfilled Jewish prophecies from the miraculous conception to His victory over death. That is positive proof that this Jesus is the promised Messiah. Some people have suggested that Jesus simply memorized the prophecies about the Messiah and then lived them out. But that idea is absurd.

Jewish Prophecy	Event	Matthew
Isaiah 7:14	Born of a virgin	1:22, 23
Micah 5:2	Place of birth	2:5, 6
Hosea 11:1	Flight to Egypt	2:15
Jeremiah 31:15	Slaughter of infants	2:16-18
Isaiah 11:1	Home in Nazareth	2:23
Isaiah 40:3	Coming of a	3:3
Malachi 3:1	forerunner to the Messiah	11:10
Isaiah 9:1, 2	Jesus' works	4:14-16
Isaiah 53:4	" "	8:17
Isaiah 42:1-4	" "	12:17-21
Isaiah 6:9, 10	Jesus' manner of	13:14, 15, 35
Psalm 78:2	speaking	
Isaiah 29:13	Jesus' opposition	15:7-9
Zechariah 9:9	Jerusalem entry	21:4, 5
Isaiah 62	" "	
Psalm 118:22	Rejection by people	21:42
Isaiah 8:14	" " "	
Zechariah 13:7	Disciples' denial	26:31

There were too many prophecies about Jesus that He could not live out. For instance, as a mere human being trying to fake being the Messiah, He could not have determined the nature of the conception, the virgin birth, His birthplace, the flight to Egypt, the slaughter of the infants, the home in Nazareth, or the opposition. It was prophesied that no bone in His body would be broken and people would cast lots for His garments. Those were not lived out by Jesus, but by Gentile soldiers who would have had no knowledge that Jewish prophecies spoke about such things.

Some people who try to dodge the fact that Jesus *is* the Messiah go so far as to suggest that all the prophecies were accidently fulfilled by Him. That's even more preposterous! Peter Stoner has mathematically calculated the probability of any one person's fulfilling even forty-eight of the sixty prophecies of the Messiah would be one in 10,000,000,000,-000,000,000,000,000,000,000,000 plus 147 more zeroes added to the end of that figure (Peter W. Stoner, *Science Speaks*, Van Kampen, 1952, p. 77). No wonder Paul said "that at the name of Jesus every every knee should bow ... and that every tongue should confess that Jesus Christ is Lord, to the glory of God the Father" (Philippians 2:10, 11).

Jesus did more than fulfill the specific prophecies about the Messiah. He also fulfilled the Jewish expectation that the Messiah would be a living fulfillment of the mission God gave to the nation of Israel. Jesus' life beautifully paralleled important aspects in the life of Israel. Matthew traced that parallel so his Jewish readers would get the point that Jesus came to head a new Israel.

Israel	Event	Jesus
Genesis 46:2, 3	Dream instructs father	Matthew 2:13
Genesis 46:7	In Egypt as a babe	Matthew 2:14
Exodus 12:40, 41 Hosea 11:1	Comes out of Egypt	Matthew 2:15
Exodus 14:21, 22 (1 Corinthians 10:1, 2)	Baptism	Matthew 3:13-17
Exodus 15:22-25	Temptation in the wilderness	Matthew 4:1-11
Exodus 19–31	God's Word given on a mountain	Matthew 5–7

Not only did Jesus fulfill Jewish prophecies about the specifics in the life of the Messiah and the Jewish expectations that the Messiah would be an extension of Israel's mission; He also absorbed all the titles that the Jews had used in their Scriptures to refer to the promised Messiah, and Matthew reveals those titles. A very interesting thing is that these titles were given to Jesus by a wide range of witnesses: blind men, Gentiles, a crowd of people, Peter, God, demons, a captain at the crucifixion, and Jesus himself. The following titles, which the prophets used hundreds of years earlier, were again all used to describe Jesus in the book of Matthew:

Son of David. 1:1; 9:27; 15:22; 20:30; 21:9

Christ. 1:1, 16; 11:2; 16:16, 20; 23:10, 26:63; 27:17

Immanuel. 1:23

9

King of the Jews. 2:2; 27:37
Ruler. 2:6
Lord. 3:3; 7:22; 8:25; 9:28; 14:28; 15:27; 18:21; 26:22
God's beloved Son. 3:17; 17:5
Teacher. 8:19; 9:11; 10:24; 17:24; 22:16, 24, 36; 26:18
Son of God. 8:29; 16:16; 27:54
Son of Man. 9:6; 11:19; 12:8; 13:41; 16:13, 27, 28; 26:24, 64
God's Servant. 12:18
Prophet. 21:11
Shepherd. 26:31

From the first sentence in his Gospel, Matthew highlighted the truth that Jesus *is* the Messiah. In fact, the word *Christ* is the Greek word for the Hebrew word *Messiah*. However, Matthew did not just identify Jesus as the Messiah for the Jews, but the Savior for all peoples.

Savior for all Peoples
A. The nobodies

Do you ever feel as if you are a nobody?

Do you ever feel as if no one notices you, no one cares, and you are making no contribution to this world? Ever feel as if God does not love you and that Jesus has no interest in being your friend?

Sure, God notices the Abrahams, Isaacs, Jacobs, Judahs, Davids, and Solomons of the world. But how about the Ediths, Ethels, Mortimers, Matildas, and Knofels? Who wants to notice people with names like those?

Well, folks, those names aren't as bad as Rehoboam, Abijah, Jotham and Jeconiah, Eliakim, Achim, and Eliud, but those people are listed in Matthew 1:2-17. And catch this— they are listed *alongside of* Abraham, Isaac, Jacob, Judah, David, and Solomon. There is not a hint that those "biggies" have more status than the "smallees."

We know about some of the "big" accomplishments of those "headliner" people, but how about all those other names that are intimately tied in with Jesus? What did those people do that were earth shaking, people moving, and situationally sensational? As far as *we* know, some of them did nothing that would warrant a promotion certificate, plaque, merit pay, applause, or even a small notation in a church paper or bulletin.

Now, take the time to read that list slowly.

To Abraham was born Isaac; and to Isaac, Jacob; and to Jacob, Judah and his brothers; and to Judah were born Perez and Zerah by Tamar; and to Perez was born Hezron; and to Hezron, Ram; and to Ram was born Amminadab; and to Amminadab, Nahshon; and to Nahshon, Salmon; and to Salmon was born Boaz by Rahab; and to Boaz was born Obed by Ruth; and to Obed, Jesse; and to Jesse was born David the king.

And to David was born Solomon by her who had been the wife of Uriah; and to Solomon was born Rehoboam; and to Rehoboam, Abijah; and to Abijah, Asa; and to Asa was born Jehoshaphat; and to Jehoshaphat, Joram; and to Joram, Uzziah; and to Uzziah was born Jotham; and to Jotham, Ahaz; and to Ahaz, Hezekiah; and to Hezekiah was born Manasseh; and to Manasseh, Amon; and to Amon, Josiah; and to Josiah were born Jeconiah and his brothers, at the time of the deportation to Babylon.

And after the deportation to Babylon, to Jeconiah was born Shealtiel; and to Shealtiel, Zerubbabel; and to Zerubbabel was born Abiud; and to Abiud, Eliakim; and to Eliakim, Azor; and to Azor was born Zadok; and to Zadok, Achim; and to Achim, Eliud; and to Eliud was born Eleazar; and to Eleazar, Matthan; and to Matthan, Jacob; and to Jacob was born Joseph the husband of Mary, by whom was born Jesus, who is called Christ.

Therefore all the generations from Abraham to David are fourteen generations; and from the deportation to Babylon to the time of Christ fourteen generations (Matthew 1:2-17).

Just try to find out some accomplishment of most of the people in that list. You won't be able to do it. Most of those people are like most of us. There is not one accomplishment that was recorded and remembered fifty years after they died. But that fact does not eliminate their worth. Nor does it eliminate our worth. Each person is worth as much as any other person.

Paul drove this point home when he said that every person is needed in the same way that every member in our physical bodies is needed. The foot is not inferior because it is not getting the attention and strokes the hand gets. The ear is not inferior because it doesn't get the compliments the eye gets.

On the other hand, the head is not superior to the feet because it has the brains. Every member in the body is valuable because it is unique and thus has something to contribute to the body that the other members do not have.

And guess what? Every human being is valuable because each person is unique. No one has ever been like you, nor will anyone ever be like you. God has given us several identifying marks that remind us about our valuable uniqueness. For instance, no one else has the same voice or set of fingerprints that you have.

Just think about all the people on earth, and multiply that number by ten (for each finger). Then remember that no two fingers have the same prints. That's a miraculous variety to squeeze into such a small space as the fingertips. God is indeed magnificent.

Your very own fingerprints is one way God reminds you about your unique individuality and thus worth.

Let's look at your uniqueness another way. A person gets one half of a cell from his father and one half of a cell from his mother. Because of genes handed down from one generation to another, each person has the potential of inheriting any physical characteristics of anyone in his ancestral family tree. If a person had a great, great, great, great grandfather who was seven feet tall, he would have a chance of being seven feet tall. If one had a grandparent 200 years ago with red and green hair, he has a chance to inherit red and green hair. The number of combinations from which a person can draw at conception is unbelievable. Someone has estimated that when a person is conceived today, he can become 1 of 240,000,000 plus 250 *billion* more zeros added on. It would take a person working full time (forty hours per week) 34,000 years just to write down the zeros. You and I are unique! That's value! And God sees that value and honors it with His love, care, and recognition. People who are unknown on earth are well known in Heaven (2 Corinthians 6:9). The listing in Matthew 1:2-17 proves it. Nobody is a nobody from Heaven's viewpoint.

Isn't it time that we started seeing people from Heaven's perspectives? One of the marks of being a new creation in Christ is that we quit recognizing people by their human position only (2 Corinthians 5:16). If Jesus is not embarrassed to show relationship with all those unknowns in that genea-logical list, then we should be willing to reach out to all kinds of people around us. Jesus didn't just declare relationships in a list; He demonstrated relationships in His life. He noticed, cared, touched, and spent time with beggars, sinners, wid-ows, common laborers, servants, and a host of "nameless" people.

B. *The moral failures.*

I can hear some of you saying, "Okay, granted, God notices the nobodies. But those must be the 'good' nobodies. How about somebody who goofs it morally? If God knew my thoughts and my past and some of the things I'm into now, He wouldn't care. I'm just not the 'good' person Abraham, Isaac, David, and Solomon were."

Take your blinders off. Those guys did some things you wouldn't dream about. Abraham pawned his wife off as his sister and let her join a harem to save his own skin—twice (Genesis 12:10-16; 20:1-18).

He himself took his wife's housemaid as a concubine (Gen-esis 16:1-6). Isaac held favoritism for one son over another (Genesis 25:28) and also pawned his wife off as his sister to save his skin (Genesis 26:1-11). Jacob cheated his brother of valuable treasures (Genesis 25:27-34; 27:18-24); he also lived in polygamy and made concubines of two of his housemaids (Genesis 27—30). Judah impregnated his daughter-in-law and thus became the biological father of his own grandchildren (Genesis 38). David had an affair with his next door neighbor and arranged to have her husband killed (2 Samuel 11). Solomon was polygamous and maintained a large harem.

Hezekiah, who was known as a righteous king, was filled with pride and failed to give God credit for God's deeds (2 Chronicles 32:25). Rahab was a prostitute in Jericho (Joshua 2:1), and she is in this listing of people Jesus identifies with (Matthew 1:5).

Does that mean that moral failure is okay? No! But it does mean that God's grace is greater than man's disgrace. It means that God does not lock us into our past.

Yesterday ended last night; so we must let it!

God specializes in picking up the broken pieces of human-ity and molding those pieces into a beautiful human mosaic.

13

We do not have to lock ourselves into the guilt of yesterday's sins. The good news (gospel) is that God knows us and yet loves us. That good news is beamed to us in Jesus, "who will save His people from their sins" (Matthew 1:21).

If Jesus is willing to identify with people who have really goofed it morally, then so should we. Someone has observed that the church is the only army that shoots its own wounded. If Abraham, Isaac, or David had sinned today the way they did in their day, would the church reach out with a ministry of reconciliation? Would we see potential? Would we offer forgiveness? Would they become recycled for fruitful ministry if they were among our fellowship today? Do we write off our list those whom God still has on His? Would we make sure they never taught a Sunday-school class or preached in our pulpit again? What a loss if God had reacted then with those failures the way some of us do today with ours. Just look at all the Psalms that would be missing from David's pen.

This genealogical list reads so boringly, but the truth that jumps out of it is so beneficial. Here are some of those truths that spring from these seemingly boring verses.

1. God is faithful to his promise. God promised the Jews a Messiah, and He kept that promise in spite of the fact that Judah and Israel had a track record of unfaithfulness to God. No wonder David saturated the Psalms with the praise of God's loving kindness and faithfulness. If God kept that promise, He will keep all His promises to us even though we disappoint Him.

2. Jesus is the Messiah the Jews had longed for.

3. God's love crosses all kinds of human barriers, as demonstrated by the categories of people in this list. This list shows that the racial barrier is crossed because both Jews and non-Jews (Rahab and Ruth) are in the list. The status barrier is crossed because both headliners and seemingly nobodies are listed. The sexual barrier is crossed because both male and female are listed. The moral barrier is crossed because those who at first appear to be righteous are listed with those who are really, at times, unrighteous.

Of course, we must not think that everyone in this list was a saved person. Some were extremely rebellious against God, and there is no indication that they ever turned their lives toward God. However, their inclusion in this genealogy suggests that they still have dignity, worth, and potential in the sight of God. God does not cease to love the unlovely. Any of these who died without God as his Lord did so because he chose not to be identified with God — not because God did not want to be identified with him.

I don't think it is accidental that Matthew begins with a list of all kinds of people and closes with a commission for us to go to all kinds of people.

> Go therefore and make disciples of all the nations, baptizing them in the name of the Father and the Son and the Holy Spirit, teaching them to observe all that I commanded you; and lo, I am with you always, even to the end of the age (Matthew 28:19, 20).

Accepting Ourselves as God Does

In this listing, somewhere, are you and I. So why is it so difficult for us to accept ourselves? We live too much of our lives feeling like nobodies because we believe we are. Why is this so?

It isn't the things that happen to us or the words said to us or about us that put us down. No human external event can determine our worth. However, our own thoughts can and do.

We live in a society in which people specialize in competing against each other and comparing ourselves with others. If we do that long enough, we will eventually put ourselves into a mental pit where we feel unworthy, unacceptable, and unproductive.

In such a society, we easily adopt many belief-systems that belittle us. Here are some of those negative and belittling belief-systems:

1. My family status makes me worth something.
2. Productivity that can be measured makes me valuable.
3. Moral perfection makes me acceptable.
4. Being accepted by people means I am loved and lovable.

But what happens to us when we don't live up to those expectations? If we are from the wrong family-line, we begin thinking that we aren't worth as much as somebody else. When we goof it at work, we begin thinking that we are not valuable. If we sin, we begin thinking that we are totally unacceptable. If we are rejected by people, we begin thinking we are unlovable. Do you know what it is that gets us down on ourselves? It is not events that have happened to us or what we have done. No human event can determine our worth. But our beliefs about those events can make us question our own worth because we talk to ourselves with those beliefs. And we do that self-talk at the rate of 1300 words a minute. Most Christians do this at one time or another in their lives. And that negative self-talk traps us to defeatism, for as a person thinks, so he is (Proverbs 23:7). That kind of negative thinking forces us to work in order to gain worth, acceptability, and value. But the more we work for acceptance, the more we face the fact that we make mistakes, and that causes us to question our worth even more.

What is needed? Not a change of human events. None of us can do anything to change events of the past nor can we do as much as we would like to control and change events that happen today. But each of us can control and change our self-talk into positive self-talk.

What is positive self-talk for God's people? In a nutshell, it is found in 1 Peter 1:18, 19, "Knowing that you were not redeemed with perishable things . . . but with precious blood . . . the blood of Christ."

Too many of us have allowed any negative self-talk to take over the speaker's platform in our minds, grab a mike, and start lecturing us at 1300 words a minute. Do you know who is really behind that? The devil is, for the devil is full of deceit and wants us to lie to ourselves that certain events mean we are unworthy. The events may be such things as goofs on the job, getting fired from the job, the rejection of a person, not getting included on somebody's invitation list, a divorce, being by-passed for a promotion, a disagreement with somebody, criticism, or someone's becoming angry with us.

As soon as the negative and deceptive self-talk begins, we need to tell ourselves, "Stop! You have no right to talk to me like that. I have not been redeemed by a perishable thing such as a promotion (or being accepted by someone, or never being criticized, or not getting fired, or whatever). I have been redeemed by the precious blood of Christ; therefore, I am loved and worth something."

Some of you right now are thinking, "But you don't know

16

me. If you knew me, you wouldn't be so positive." But a person just like you can be found in verses 2-16 of Matthew one.

Our need is to accept God's acceptance of us even if we feel unacceptable. The key is to surrender our thoughts so they become captive to the way God thinks. We must destroy false speculations that deceive us and others.

> We are destroying speculations and every lofty thing raised us against the knowledge of God, and we are taking every thought captive to the obedience of Christ (2 Corinthians 10:5).

We need to fill our thoughts with the positive, and the the peace of God will fill us.

The Need:
> Finally, brethren, whatever is true, whatever is honorable, whatever is right, whatever is pure, whatever is lovely, whatever is of good repute, if there is any excellence and if anything worthy of praise, let your mind dwell on these things (Philippians 4:8).

The Promise:
> ". . . and the God of peace shall be with you" (Philippians 4:9).

Conclusion

God's people are on God's list just as surely today as they were in Jesus' day in spite of lack of human accomplishments that are recorded, family lines, race, sex, or moral imperfections.

When we say to ourselves, "I'm not worth anything," we should stop that talk and hear God say, "You *are* worthy." And when we argue with God, "Prove it, God," we need to be open to hear Him say, "O.K., I will. I created you in My image. That makes you worthy. I bought you. That makes you worthy. I have adopted you. That makes you worthy. I allowed my Son to die for you. That makes you worthy. I am preparing a place for you. That makes you worthy. I am coming back for you. That makes you worthy."

When we reply, "But what have I done to deserve it?" The answer is, "Not one thing!" What has a child done to earn the love of the parents after the birth of that child? Nothing! But the parents love the child of worth. And so it is with us and God. And so it was with all those on that list. Both the well known *on earth* and the unknown *on earth* have this in common. They are equally well known in Heaven.

God says to His people today what He said to His people in ancient days:

> But now thus says the Lord, your Creator, O Jacob, and He who formed you, O Israel, "Do not fear, for I have redeemed you; I have called you by name; you are Mine! When you pass through the waters, I will be with you; and through the rivers, they will not overflow you. When you walk through the fire, you will not be scorched, nor will the flame burn you. For I am the Lord your God, The Holy One of Israel, your Savior; I have given Egypt as your ransom, Cush and Seba in your place. Since you are precious in My sight, since you are honored and I love you, I will give other men in your place and other peoples in exchange for your life."
>
> Do not call to mind the former things, or ponder things of the past. Behold, I will do something new (Isaiah 43:1-4, 18, 19).

That makes us worthy of being on His list. Now let's accept it, thank God, and praise Him for it—and open that list to others as we reach out to them with our love and acceptance.

The Royal Family

(Matthew 1:18-21)

The Nature of Jesus' Coming

Now the birth of Jesus Christ was as follows. When His mother Mary had been betrothed to Joseph, before they came together she was found to be with child by the Holy Spirit (Matthew 1:18).

Now all this took place that what was spoken by the Lord through the prophet might be fulfilled, saying, "Behold the virgin shall be with child, and shall bear a son, and they shall call His name Immanuel," which translated means, "God with us" (Matthew 1:22, 23).

And [he] kept her a virgin until she gave birth to a Son; and he called His name Jesus (Matthew 1:25).

God could have sent Jesus to earth in any form God chose. But God chose for Jesus to come in human form and promised it centuries in advance.

And I will put enmity between you and the woman, and between your seed and her seed; He shall bruise you on the head, and you shall bruise him on the heel (Genesis 3:15).

God could have sent Jesus as an angel or as a fully mature human being. But God chose for Jesus to be born as a baby and grow into manhood. There are several applications we can make about this human-infant-growth nature of Jesus' coming. We'll consider two important ones here, His humility and His identity with us.

A. His Humility

The popular flow of life is to move from one plateau of

status to a higher position of status. We all look forward to promotions, not demotions. But Jesus voluntarily chose demotion for the benefit of mankind.

> Who, although He existed in the form of God, did not regard equality with God a thing to be grasped, but emptied Himself, taking the form of a bond-servant, and being made in the likeness of men. And being found in appearance as a man, He humbled Himself by becoming obedient to the point of death, even death on a cross (Philippians 2:6-8).

Jesus "emptied Himself." What humility! But humility is not to stop with Jesus. We are told, "Have this attitude in yourselves which was also in Christ Jesus" (Philippians 2:5). That does not mean that we are to walk around with a terminal case of inferiority complex, hosting our own pity party. Toward the end of Jesus' ministry, He told people to love others as themselves (Matthew 22:39). Years later Paul wrote that husbands should love their wives as they do their own bodies (Ephesians 5:28). God does not want us to throw hate darts at ourselves. To help prevent us from hating ourselves, God offers us grace in the package of forgiveness (which wipes out our past), His Holy Spirit (who equips our present), and hope (which assures our future). God accepts our past, present, and future. That means He accepts us; so cancel the pity party.

If emptying self doesn't mean we are to be infected with inferiority, then what does it mean? It means we quit thinking of ourselves more highly than we ought to think (Romans 12:3). It means we pull the plug on an inflated case of ego and let it drain out of our inner man. It means allowing Christ to be more than the invited resident inside of us but also to be the president—or rather, king—of our lives.

It means that we recognize that without Christ we are nothing. The impotency of individual Christians can be traced to a dependency upon self strength and not upon God's power. We spend too much time trying to live *for* Christ rather than living *by* His indwelling power. The challenge of being a disciple of Jesus is to envision, plan, and start practicing what we cannot do on our own strength and resources. When we humble ourselves enough to do that, we will discover that the power released on the day of Pentecost did not die in the first century.

Paul learned that lesson well. He thought he had to have human strength to channel God's ministry and make it succeed, but God said, "My grace is sufficient for you, for power is perfected in weakness."

Paul responded,

Most gladly, therefore, I will rather boast about my weaknesses, that the power of Christ may dwell in me. Therefore I am well content with weaknesses, with insults, with distresses, with persecutions, with difficulties, for Christ's sake; for when I am weak, then I am strong (2 Corinthians 12:9, 10).

I confess to you that I have lived too much of my life depending only upon my own ability, energy, stamina, schemes, and workaholic kind of activities. God could have died during those days and I would not have missed Him from among the resources I had been relying upon.

During that period of my life, I discovered an essential truth. When I was strong in myself, I was really weak. What I needed was to admit Knofel's impotency and God's power. I had to deny myself and affirm the inner Christ as the only source for living.

B. *His Identity With Us*

Someone has suggested that we should never judge anyone until we have walked in his shoes. Jesus walked in our shoes when he put on flesh. He understands what we go through from the time we struggle for that first breath as an infant until we grab for that last breath before death. He went through those passages of life that we go through.

He depended upon His mother for milk and affection. No doubt, He knew what it meant to be accepted, cuddled, changed, sung to, smiled at, and rocked. I imagine He went through those "terrible two's" when He wrestled with that burning issue, "Who's boss around here anyway?"

He lived probably through some "touch and go" years during which everything He saw was an opportunity to start something, but nothing was worth finishing. And those adolescent years? Yes! He matured through those also. It appears

He even tried his wings as an "adult" before being one, but drew back and submitted to his parents (Luke 2:41-52).

He had brothers and sisters and all that goes along with that. According to tradition, He knew about losing an earthly parent to death and then becoming the bread-and-butter provider for the family. He also experienced leaving home for an unselfish ministry. In that ministry, He lived through everything anyone would experience in a ministry or vocation. He had times of acceptance and rejection, of being honored and threatened, of being understood and misunderstood, of being appreciated and taken for granted, of being voted for and voted against, of having friends and losing friends, of having family support and having family opposition. He was lonely, tired, hungry, broke, and angry.

He was even tempted in every way we are, yet without sin (Hebrews 4:15).

The songs that say, "I must tell Jesus," and, "What a friend we have in Jesus," are right on target. Jesus is a friend who knows what we are going through. We can tell it to Him, for He understands. He has felt your hurts and aches. His empathy stretches across time, for He still feels *with* us—not just *for* us.

So when Jesus says, "Follow Me," He knows it can be done. He's been there. He's not like the second lieutenant who gives orders to master sergeants about something the lieutenant knows nothing about at the hands-on level. Jesus' love is with identity and understanding.

The Parental Selection

We have four children at home—Randy, Rena, Rhonda, and Rachel. And we have another "R" name picked out—just in case. "Rover." Julia and I have made a will in which we have designated a family to have custody of our kids should something happen to both of us. But selecting someone requires a tough decision.

Whom would you choose to become stand-in parents for you? What experience, value system, provision, character, age, and other criteria would you list? Would you want a couple with some kind of track record for child-care? Would you want someone with a steady income and financial management abilities? Would you choose a couple who, when

22

they first heard you say that you are thinking about them, would respond positively with, "Great, we would love to take your kids"? Would you want a couple who seemed to have a pretty solid marriage and settled in the community?

When God looked around for a couple to take the custody of His only Son, He chose a couple that most social workers today would reject. While we depend so much upon outward appearances, God looks upon the heart. While we want a read-out on a person's proven proficiency, God considers a person's potential.

What kind of couple did God choose? He chose a young teenage couple who were not even married and may have had no experience in child-care. I used to see Mary in her later twenties or early thirties when the angel appeared to her. But I think I was mistaken.

In those days, girls were engaged between the ages of nine and eleven to boys who were seventeen to nineteen. The engagement lasted for one year (no more and no less), and then the couple was married. If a girl was not engaged by her twelfth birthday, she was considered to be a social misfit. There is no evidence in either Scripture or other historical records that Mary had that stigma. So Mary was probably no older than twelve (really just under twelve) when she was engaged to Joseph.

That couple did not have a steady marriage, experience as parents in rearing children, proven financial management skills, or even moderate provisions. At first, it seems, neither Mary nor Joseph responded positively to God's selection of them.

Joseph did have a job as was required of all teenage boys. But his income level today would not even be in the lower-middle-class bracket. He would probably be listed in the lower-lower level and would qualify for food stamps. We know that because the material offering the couple gave after the birth of Jesus was two birds—the offering allowed for poverty-level families. But God looked beyond the surface and saw character. God chose Mary and Joseph with the same perception He used to choose David as king,

But the Lord said to Samuel, "Do not look at his appearance or at the height of his stature, because I have rejected him; for God

23

sees not as man sees, for man looks at the outward appearance, but the Lord looks at the heart (1 Samuel 16:7).

What kind of character did God see in the hearts of Mary and Joseph?

A. The Heart of Mary

At first, Mary was greatly disturbed by the news. Mary could easily have decided that she had more to lose than to gain. She could lose her trusting relationship with her parents, her reputation in the synagogue and community at large, her fiancee, and even her life.

Can't you hear Mary breaking the news to her mother:

"Mother, please sit down, I need to talk with you. Mother, I have what may sound like bad news to you and good news."

"Oh, Mary. It is so good to talk with you. You are so sensible. You have never given me a day of trouble. What is it my daughter?"

"Mother, I am pregnant." *A long silence as the two stare at each other. The mother starts to wring her hands. Shock fills her eyes while tears start down her cheeks.*

"Mary, how could you? The marriage is months away. Couldn't you wait?"

"Mother, here's the good news. I am still a virgin."

"Oh, come on, Mary. I wasn't born yesterday!"

"But it's true Mother. You see, the Holy Spirit has done this to me. Isn't that good news?"

Now how many of you mothers would fall for a line like that right away? We have three daughters at home, and I have already decided that if one of them tries that on me, I'm going to say, "No dice, baby."

Getting her folks to accept the news was just part of what had troubled Mary. How was she going to convince Joseph?

"Joseph, I'm going to have a baby."

"Oh, I know you will, Mary. We certainly do want children. God will bless us with children after we are married."

"But Joseph, I am going to have a baby before we are married."

"Oh no you aren't, Mary. We are not violating our engagement vows."

"Joseph, I'm already pregnant."

24

"What are you talking about, Mary. We haven't shared sexual love."

"I know, Joseph, but I am with child, and I'm not going to name Him after you."

"Who's the father, Mary?"

"There is no earthly father, Joseph. An angel appeared to me. I am with child of the Holy Spirit."

"Mary, what in the world have you been drinking?"

"It's true, Joseph."

"No, it's not! You are either kidding me in your jestful way, or you are with child by one of the fellows in the village. I just don't believe it!"

Not only was Mary's reputation in jeopardy, but also her acceptance in the community was on the line. How was she going to react to the stares and whispers when she went to the marketplace and the synagogue in a maternity dress as an unwed person?

Mary's life was even at stake. In those days, an engagement was as binding as a marriage. There were only two ways a Jewish couple could break an engagement. One way was by the death of one of the engaged. When that happened, the survivor was referred to as a widow or widower. The other way to break an engagement was by a legal bill of divorce, which freed both to marry someone else.

During the engagement period, each was legally committed to be sexually faithful. If either violated that, he/she was considered to be guilty of adultery. If the girl was unfaithful, the law permitted her to be stoned to death. Pregnancy, with the subsequent bodily changes, prevented a girl from claiming innocence.

Mary pondered all that in her heart, but she pondered God's greatness above the circumstance. So she transferred her fear into faithfulness. She responded with the most beautiful response anyone can give to God, "Behold the bondslave of the Lord; be it done to me according to your word" (Luke 1:38).

In that response, Mary was saying, "Regardless of what my friends and relatives may say; regardless of my personal plans; regardless of my own desires; if God's Word says to do something, I will do it—even if I do not understand."

I can't help but think that such a model made such a significant impact on the boy Jesus that He grew into manhood with
an identical commitment—to do God's will regardless of reactions surrounding Him. I wonder what kind of world this
would be if every child could grow up with such a model in
his mother. Of course, we cannot expect that kind of model in
non-Christians, but I'm afraid we do not even have it among
church families. So we fuss and fight about traditions for
which we do not have a "thus saith the Lord." Could that be
one reason some kids grow up with little respect for God's
Word? For what difference does it make whether God said
something if we are going to do what we want to do anyway?

Mary modeled humble obedience. That was her greatness.

There is another aspect of Mary's greatness that we easily
overlook. That has to do with the kind of mother she was for
her other children when she knew the privileged status of
Jesus. She treasured in her heart all the things surrounding
the birth of Jesus, which included all the shepherds had
shared (Luke 2:19). As Jesus grew, she knew about His unusual abilities such as His time with teachers in the temple
when he was only twelve, and she "treasured all these things
in her heart" (Luke 2:51).

However, there is no evidence that she gave Jesus preferen-
tial treatment over the other children. The people in Jesus'
home town could not see that He got any special treatment at
home that was different from what the other kids received.

Is not this the carpenter's son? Is not His mother called Mary, and
His brothers, James and Joseph and Simon and Judas? And His
sisters, are they not all with us? Where then did this man get all
these things (Matthew 13:55, 56)?

Mary could have played the comparing game by making
the other kids feel inferior because they were not just like
Jesus, but she evidently did not. Mary understood that every
child is unique and valuable in his own individuality. He
doesn't have to become like someone else to feel He has
worth and can make a contribution to life. Every parent
should walk in that same kind of wisdom.

Although Jesus' half brothers and sisters were uncomfortable seeing Him as the Messiah until after the resurrection,

there is no evidence that they were uncomfortable with Him as their brother. They were not filled with jealousy, nor did they feel put down by Him. In fact, they had the love, respect, and concern for Him that motivated them to want to take Him back home with them when they thought He was going off the deep end that could lead Him into trouble (Mark 3:21, 31). They certainly never had the reaction. "Let Him lie in the bed He's made. He never cared about us and Mother. He was always Mother's favorite; so let's just leave Him alone."

What delightfully wonderful interpersonal relationships must have gone on in that home. Much of the credit belongs to Mary, who knew how to treasure things in her heart without making issues out of them.

B. The heart of Joseph

Joseph probably did not at first believe that Mary was pregnant. But when Mary's body began to change, he could not deny it. Did he then believe her explanation about it? No! Joseph did not buy Mary's "good news/bad news" line. So he decided to "put her away secretly," which is a technical way of saying "divorce her quietly." That was big hearted of Joseph, because he could have publicly denied being the father and ordered Mary to be executed for unfaithfulness.

However, Joseph was not the kind of guy who made up his mind never to change it again. Some men think it is a sign of weakness to take a stand and then back down on it. You know the type: "Don't confuse me with the facts; I've already made up my mind." But Joseph, who was a model of a real macho man (not the secular, popularized cheap mutation of one), didn't think like that at all.

God's angel filled Joseph in with the facts. "Joseph, son of David, do not be afraid to take Mary as your wife; for that which has been conceived in her is of the Holy Spirit" (Matthew 1:20).

Probably with some egg on his face, Joseph surely admitted to Mary that she was right and he was wrong. That is not easy for a man to do, but it is essential for healthy relationships to continue. That takes humility. It is the kind of model that a boy growing up needs to see in the man of the house. I suspect that Joseph's humility and willingness to obey God's

27

Word even when it contradicted inner feelings, past positions, and scientific norms impacted Jesus more than we have recognized.

Joseph's modeling for Jesus didn't stop on that occasion. Everytime we see Joseph, he is making decisions for the good of his family. He knew how to deny himself for the benefit of others. As a teenage carpenter, he would just have got his business feet on the ground when he went to Bethlehem, where Jesus was born. We aren't sure why he stayed in Bethlehem instead of returning to Nazareth. However, we may not be too far off to suggest that Joseph wanted to spare Mary the wagging tongues that certainly were in high gear. His love for Mary was a protecting love, never a condescending love.

Within two years, Joseph would just have got his feet on the ground again when it was time to move the family again. In order to kill the Messiah, Herod ordered that all male children in Bethlehem who were two years old and under should be exterminated. Bethlehem was not a large town; so it would not have been difficult for Herod's officials to search and find those little tots. So Joseph left his income, house, and community for the good of his family.

Too often today, men move their families from one place to another with what seems to be little regard for the other members of the families. Too often, an advance in status and economy appear to be the overriding motives.

The next time Joseph moved, he gave up his personal preference for a place to live for God's preference—and again for the welfare of his family (Matthew 2:21-23). During Jesus' significant developmental years, He had moved three times. But good interpersonal relationships with the family compensated for early rootlessness. He was deeply rooted in the loving environment of a happy family.

There are three other aspects of Joseph's life that we can infer were tremendously positive models for Jesus. Joseph did not excuse himself from making financial sacrifices for God's kingdom because of his poverty (Luke 2:23, 24). Jesus grew up observing his parents' trusting God for their daily bread. No wonder He spoke so much about depending upon God, generosity, and the low priority for accumulating things for security. Joseph led his family in regularly keeping the religious traditions (Luke 2:41). No wonder we read that it was Jesus' custom to attend the synagogue (Luke 4:16).

Joseph was not a workaholic, long-range father, who kept his skills to himself. Joseph, the carpenter, evidently taught his son the art of carpentry (Mark 6:3). He was a father who poured himself into his son. The time he spent with his son surely helped his son have a good self-image, allowed him not to be threatened by males, allowed him to be comfortable working closely with his male disciples without being threatened teaching them what he knew and provided him a hands-on model for leading and motivating and passing on skills to others.

Although Jesus was born with meager material resources, He was in a rich family. His family was rich in love, acceptance, caring, sharing, sacrifice, and unity.

That royal family of Jesus is an example that deserves our imitation today:

1. The mother followed the Word of God regardless of any potential negative consequences.

2. The father obeyed the Word of God even when it contradicted his feelings and logical reasoning.

3. The parents did not complain about poverty or thought the world owed them something because of their privileged status.

4. The parents did not show favoritism toward their special Son.

5. There was diversity but concern and unity displayed among the brothers and sisters.

6. The father taught his skills to his son.

7. The father and mother made religious worship a custom in their family.

8. The father made self-sacrificing decisions for the benefit of the family.

9. The husband protected the wife.

That was a wealthy family that had an inheritance to pass on that could not be diminished with a stock market crash. Our kids are our heirs. What will *they* inherit?

God With Us
(Matthew 1:22-25)

Anyone want to become a worm or a snake?

When Jesus put on flesh, He demonstrated to us an empathy and love that surpasses understanding or human duplication. It was as humble for Him to do that as it would be for us to put on the skin and form of a snake or worm to crawl around in their environment, experiencing all they experience and demonstrate to them that we really understand and love them.

We are not worms. We are humans made in the image of God, but we have goofed it. Nevertheless, God came in flesh to say, "So what! I am bigger than your goofs. I still love you. Instead of rejecting you because you are not like me, I'll put on your skin and crawl around in your environment to show you that I am willing to identify with you, empathize with you, and love you."

Although Matthew began his good news by showing that Jesus had a human lineage, he quickly revealed that Jesus was more than human. Jesus' humanness is rooted in the fact that He had a human mother. His divinity is rooted in the fact that He had a superhuman Father.

The Miraculous Conception

He had a natural birth with a supernatural conception, "for that which has been conceived in her is of the Holy Spirit" (Matthew 1:20).

Mary remained a virgin until after Jesus' birth day. Joseph "kept her until she gave birth to a son . . ." (Matthew 1:25). The word *until* puts a time limit on Mary's virginity. She remained a virgin only throughout her first pregnancy.

Elsewhere we are told that Jesus had brothers and sisters (Matthew 13:55, 56). Some, who teach the theory that Mary remained a virgin until death, suggest that these were Joseph's children by a former marriage. However, there is no support for that theory. We read nothing about children accompanying Joseph and Mary to Bethlehem or Egypt. No other children seemed to be with Joseph and Mary when they took Jesus to the temple when He was twelve years old.

To suggest that Mary and Joseph had proper intimate relations after Jesus' birth does not lower our esteem for Mary. The "act of love" between a husband and wife is not dirty or vile. God created sex with married partners in mind. Sexual intimacy is a God-designed act of oneness within marriage (Genesis 2:24); it is a close personal communication that was described by the phrasing "knowing" each other (Genesis 4:1 in KJV or RSV); a way to relieve tension (Genesis 24:67); a way to share pleasure (Genesis 18:12); the means to participate in God's act of creating new life, which God commanded Adam and Eve to do (Genesis 1:28); and environment for verbally expressing appreciation for each other (Song of Solomon); a way to meet God-created human need in our mates that is a debt for husbands and wives to pay (1 Corinthians 7:2-4); and a God given protection against the onslaught of the devil (1 Corinthians 7:5). Paul commanded that husbands and wives stop depriving each other of sexual intimacy (1 Corinthians 7:5). To suppose that Mary deprived her husband throughout their married life together might tend to lower our estimation of her rather than raise it.

The magnificence of Mary is not found in a doctrine of perpetual virginity. We are not to worship Mary, but the Master. However, we should give Mary the respect due her. Her obedience, humility, risk-taking, devotion, and dedication were obvious—as well as her competence as a wife and mother. While we do not have to worship Mary to honor her, neither do we have to ignore her in order to keep from worshiping her. Many in the Protestant world have given more attention to Dorcas, Priscilla, Mary Magdalene, the woman at the Samaritan well, and the sisters of Lazarus than to Jesus' mother. Mary became the human vessel God enlisted for His visit to planet earth.

Some like to question the virgin conception because only

31

Matthew and Luke record anything about it. If such a miraculous event had really happened, they say, it would have been known to Mark, John, and Paul.

Mark, John, and Paul did know about the miraculous conception. We can tell by the way they wrote. The fact that they did not mention the word *virgin* is insignificant.

Mark began his record with the ministry of John the Baptist. Since he did not mention Jesus' birth at all, he did not have occasion to mention the miraculous conception. But note how carefully Mark mentions "the son of Mary" in recording what the neighbors in Nazareth said (Mark 6:3). Matthew recorded that the neighbors said "the carpenter's son" (Matthew 13:55) without stopping to explain that Jesus was not really the son of Joseph. Matthew did not need to explain that or say "son of Mary" because he had already made it clear that Jesus was begotten by the Holy Spirit. However, Mark had not written about that. If he had recorded "the carpenter's son" some of his readers who had not read Matthew might think that Joseph begot Jesus. So Mark carefully quoted "the son of Mary" because he was very much acquainted with the facts of the virgin conception.

And did John know about the miraculous conception? Of course he did. It is clear that John knew Jesus did not come into the world by an ordinary means when he wrote, "In the beginning was the Word, and the Word was with God, and the Word was God. He was in the beginning with God . . ." (John 1:1, 2, 14).

It is also clear that Paul knew about the miraculous conception from his recordings:

> He is the image of the invisible God, the first-born of all creation. For by Him all things were created, both in the heavens and on earth, visible and invisible, whether thrones or dominions or rulers or authorities—all things have been created by Him and for Him. And He is before all things, and in Him all things hold together (Colossians 1:15-17).

Jesus certainly could not have been before all things and created them if He were begotten by Joseph after creation. Nor could God have "sent His Son" if His Son did not exist until a human conception with Joseph as His father.

32

Although the other Biblical writers did not refer to it, they surely accepted the fact that Jesus' conception fulfilled the prophecy of Isaiah, "Behold the virgin shall be with child . . ." (Isaiah 7:14; Matthew 1:23).

We do not understand the "how" of it any more than Mary did. But the angel's message is still the best answer: "For nothing will be impossible with God" (Luke 1:37).

However, we can understand the "why" of it. When man first sinned, God promised Jesus when He said to the disguised devil, "And I will put enmity between you and the woman, and between your seed and her seed; He shall bruise you in the head, and you shall bruise him on the heel" (Genesis 3:15). Mary's son fulfilled that promise. That's the reason He was named Jesus. *Jesus* means *Savior.* He came to save people from their sins (Matthew 1:21).

The Holy Spirit and Jesus

To be born of a woman by the Holy Spirit makes Jesus unique. He is one of a kind. He is the only God-man. He is God's perfect man, as He humbled himself, put on flesh, and became obedient to death without sin. He is also man's perfect God. He said, "I and the Father are one" (John 10:30). "He who has seen Me has seen the Father" (John 14:9).

To be begotten by the Holy Spirit is to be begotten by God. For the Holy Spirit is the extended earthly presence of God. This is made clear in the Old Testament as well as the New Testament.

The Hebrews often taught by using a literary device called parallelism. A parallelism is saying something one way and then saying the same thing in a slightly different way. Words that are paralleled mean the same thing. Notice the parallelism between the italicized words below:

"Do not *cast me away from Thy presence* and do not *take Thy Holy Spirit from me*" (Psalm 51:11).

"Cast me away from" is paralleled with "take from me." "Thy Holy Spirit" is paralleled with "thy presence."

Where can I *go* from Thy *Spirit?* Or where can I *flee* from Thy *presence?* (Psalm 139:7).

Notice that "go" and "flee" parallel and "Spirit" and "presence" parallel.

Where the Holy Spirit is, there is the presence of God. That's why Peter could say to Ananias that he lied to the Holy Spirit in one sentence and then say two sentences later that he lied to God (Acts 5:3, 4). The Holy Spirit is the extended presence of God.

That helps us understand Jesus' teaching. In John 14:16, Jesus promised the coming of "another Helper." The word *another* means another of exactly the same kind. The same kind as who? As Jesus had been. That helper is referred to as the *Spirit* in verse 17. But in verse 18 Jesus said "*I* will come to you." In verse 20, He said, "*I* in you." Then in verse 23, He refers to both *himself* and the *Father* when He says, "We will come . . . and make Our abode with him."

Notice that Jesus spoke about the coming of the Holy Spirit, himself, and the Father. That's because the three are inseparable. The coming of one brings the presence of the others.

So it is fitting that when we read that Jesus was conceived by Mary of the Holy Spirit, we also read, "And they shall call His name Immanuel, which translated means, 'God with us'" (Matthew 1:23).

The magnificence of Jesus is that He was both fully human (born of a woman) and fully God (begotten by the Holy Spirit).

God With Us
The Bible is clear that Jesus was God in flesh.

"What was from the beginning, what we have heard, what we have seen with our eyes, what we beheld and our hands handled, concerning the Word of Life—and the life was manifested, and we have seen and bear witness and proclaim to you the eternal life, which was with the Father and was manifested to us—what we have seen and heard we proclaim to you also, that you also may have fellowship with us; and indeed our fellowship is with the Father, and with His Son Jesus Christ (1 John 1:1-3).

Namely, that God was in Christ reconciling the world to himself, not counting their trespasses against them, and He has committed to us the word of reconciliation (2 Corinthians 5:19).

34

And we know that the Son of God has come, and has given us understanding, in order that we might know Him who is true, and we are in Him who is true, in His Son Jesus Christ. This is the true God and eternal life (1 John 5:20).

The same titles that are ascribed to God the Father are ascribed to Jesus, such as Lord, Savior, Redeemer, Shepherd, Creator, and only Sovereign.

We do not know how three can be one. However, we do not have to understand that. God's ways and His thoughts are as far above ours as the heavens are above the earth. We do not even understand the ways of planet earth with all of our sophisticated scientific equipment. So why argue about those facts about God we do not understand? I am glad we do not fully understand God, for then He would cease to be God. Whatever we can fully understand, we can master. No human will ever be able to master God. He was, is, and will always be the Lord God Almighty. He's mightier than all.

For those who want to have some kind of handle on the Trinity, perhaps the following may help. However, the following can never fully explain how the Father, Son, and Holy Spirit can be three and yet one. Nevertheless, here are three feeble attempts.

(1) Water is three-in-one: H_2O.

(2) I am three-in-one: I am a father, a son, and a husband — all three. Each of these has distinct functions, yet I am one.

(3)

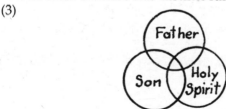

What overlaps may be seen as the identicals of the Father, Son and Holy Spirit. While what does not overlap may be seen as the distinctiveness of the three. The distinctiveness is not absorbed by the oneness and the oneness does not eliminate the distinctiveness of each one. Perhaps what overlaps are the essence and character of each, which are identical, while what does not overlap are the distinct functions of each.

Application of "God With Us"

We can get too bogged down mentally wrestling with the philosophical understanding of Jesus' being "God with us" and miss the practical application of it.

Since Jesus is "God with us," then to follow Jesus is to follow God. To see how Jesus acts and reacts is to observe God's acting and reacting.

To hear Jesus is to hear God.

That means we had better listen more carefully and put into practice what He teaches.

Jesus is referred to as the Alpha and Omega—the first and the last. Alpha and Omega are the first and last letters in the Greek alphabet. Not only will God (Jesus) have the last *word* to say in history, He will also have the last *letter*. When He finishes speaking, no one, regardless of status or earned degrees, will have even one little letter to add, let alone a word, sentence, or paragraph. Our theology and theories are finished when He says His last letter.

To get ready for that, we should quit arguing with Him now. Let us now take the position, "If Jesus said it, that settles it. I believe it and will do it." That is the practical application of Matthew's beginning his record stating that Jesus is "God with us."

So let us read the rest of Matthew with more attention. Let us see the footprints of God, hear the voice of God, feel the heartbeat of God, and see the outreached hands of God. And then let's allow His feet to slip into our shoes, His voice to fill our throats, His heartbeat to regulate ours, and His hands to be at the ends of our arms.

Then and only then do we begin to catch on to the significance of "and they shall call His name Immanuel; which translated means, 'God with us'" (Matthew 1:23).

The question is—are you letting God be with you? Or are you a *"Burger King"* Christian"—trying to have it *your* way and not His?

36

Check Your COMMITMENT

Studies from Matthew

4

by Knofel Staton

Jesus for Us

(Matthew 3, 4)

It is not enough to have someone live with us unless he also lives for us. And there is a big difference between living *with* someone and living *for* someone. We have mice that live with us, but they surely don't live for us nor do we live for them.

The presence of Jesus is not only "God with us," but also "God for us." We see that at the outset of His ministry—at His baptism.

The Messenger

He came out of the wilderness looking and smelling more like an animal than a man. He roasted grasshoppers and popped them into his mouth as if they were peanuts. Not many of us today would invite him to teach our Sunday school class because of the way he dressed, nor invite him to our basket dinner because of what he might bring.

But John was God's man referred to by Isaiah the prophet: "The voice of one crying in the wilderness. Make ready the way of the Lord, make His paths straight" (Matthew 3:3).

The ministry of John signaled the imminent presence of the King. In those days, a person was assigned the task of running ahead of a king's caravan to pick up debris and to fill in holes so the king's ride would be smoother. At the same time, this person would verbally announce "The king is coming! The king is coming!" The forerunner prepared the entrance of the king. That was John the Baptist's task.

God's Messiah was to be revealed, and some changes needed to take place—not on the rocky roads, but in stony hearts.

So John came preaching a message of change—repentance.

The interesting thing is that John called for the insiders—God's people—to repent, not the outsiders. Is it possible that we who are God's people do not take seriously enough the continuous mandate that we, too, are to be changing daily? To Christians, Paul wrote, "Be transformed by the renewing of your mind" (Romans 12:2). Too often we might as well sing, "Just as I am I'll come, and just as I am I'll remain until He comes again." John's message was not just change for change's sake, but rather change because the kingdom of God was at hand. The "kingdom of God" is a phrase that primarily refers to the rulership of God.

When we pray, "Thy kingdom come," we are praying, "Thy will be done on earth as it is in Heaven."

But to allow God's rule to reign requires that we be willing to change.

Jesus needed hearts willing to change in order for God to do an effective work in and through people. That is still what He needs. The greatest hindrance to Jesus' ministry today is not the opposing outsider, but the obstinate insider. I have discovered that people who will not change will not because they think they are always right. And the person who thinks he is always right eventually becomes more of a competitor against God than a complementary companion with God. Unchanging people are more *in* the way than *on* the way.

Jesus gave John the finest compliment given to any human, "Truly I say to you, among those born of women there has not arisen anyone greater than John the Baptist . . ." (Matthew 11:11). John was great because he gave himself away in service to the Master by preparing hearts to receive Jesus.

You and I can become John the Baptists today. We too can prepare the royal road by offering ourselves to change whatever is in people's hearts that prevents the entrance of Jesus. We can be used by God's Spirit to lift some valleys (discouragement, feelings of worthlessness, neglect, rejection), lower some mountains (arrogance, feelings of self-sufficiency), and smooth some rough roads (removing rocks of misunderstanding, bitterness, and grudges). But we cannot do that for others if we remain isolated from them. We need to be willing to become friends with people and let them observe some valleys in our lives that have been raised, some mountains that have been lowered, and stones that have been removed.

And when they wonder why, they can hear us announce, "The King has come—and He is still coming."

John's greatness is also seen in the fact that he turned the spotlight off himself to Jesus. When people wanted to put John's name on the marquee, he took it down and put Jesus' up. John's philosophy was, "He must increase, but I must decrease" (John 3:30). John made it clear that he was just a messenger while Jesus was the Master.

John was the fulfillment of God's long-established plan to send an Elijah in front of Jesus. John did not realize he was that significant. "'What then? Are You Elijah?' And he said, 'I am not'" (John 1:21). I wonder how many times God uses us in more significant roles than we understand or admit. It is probably a protection to our egos that we do not know. Too many people boast of their significance and force that significance upon others. "I am God's prophet! I am God's Elijah!" John left the titles for others.

Jesus admitted that John was that Elijah-type person that God had promised long ago. "And if you care to accept it, he himself is Elijah, who was to come" (Matthew 11:14).

What was there about John and Elijah that connected them?

1. Both their backgrounds are obscure. We know only where Elijah lived and who John's parents were.

2. Both challenged religious leaders of the day.

3. Both upset female members of royal families—Jezebel and Herodias.

4. Both spent time in the wilderness.

5. Both preached about contemporary ethical issues.

6. Both were forerunners—Elijah of eighth century B.C. prophets and John of Jesus.

7. Both preached at times when pagan philosophies were prevalent—in Elijah's time it was Baal; in John's it was the Epicureans and the Stoics.

8. Both were courageously bold.

9. Both wore strange clothing.

10. Both called for repentance.

The Master

The extraordinary humility of King Jesus shone when He approached His forerunner. No king would have given his forerunner any recognition, let alone ask him for a favor in front of a crowd of people who had gathered to hear the king's name acclaimed.

But instead of coming to the crowd to receive their blessings, Jesus came to John to receive John's baptism.

Jesus' action was so shocking that we still have a tough time believing it. In fact, it was somewhat of an embarrassing action. It embarrasses us when we stubbornly refuse baptism because of tradition, shyness, thinking we are good enough without it, or not understanding everything about it. It has been embarrassing enough that scholars still argue the reason.

By making baptism His first public act, He taught us that He is a surprising Messiah. He refused then and refuses today to be restricted to the little theological boxes we think we have Him trapped in.

From man's standpoint, Jesus was the only one there with a legitimate reason not to be baptized. But God had reasons that went beyond man's. Here are some of those reasons.

To fulfill righteousness. John was shocked when he saw Jesus come out of the crowd to be baptized in the Jordan. At first, he even refused to baptize Jesus. "But John tried to prevent Him, saying, 'I have need to be baptized by You, and do You come to me?'" But Jesus refused to be refused. "Permit it at this time; for in this way it is fitting for us to fulfill all righteousness" (Matthew 3:14, 15).

What did Jesus mean by fulfilling all righteousness? The Greek word for righteousness was originally used to refer to the quality of conforming to a given standard—of obeying the rules. It later came to refer to right relationships. Right relationships are broken when we refuse any standards that keep us identified with each other. Faith, repentance, and baptism identify us with God and with the people of God. That is clear from Galatians 3:26-29.

For you are all sons of God through faith in Christ Jesus. *[Identity with God.]* For all of you who were baptized into Christ have clothed yourselves with Christ. *[Identity with Christ.]* There is neither Jew nor Greek, there is neither slave nor free man, there is neither male nor female; for you are all one in Christ Jesus. And if you belong to Christ, then you are Abraham's offspring, heirs according to promise. *[Identity with God's people.]*

That relationship with God and God's people is seen on the first day the church began:

> And Peter said to them, "Repent, and let each of you be baptized in the name of Jesus Christ for the forgiveness of your sins; and you shall receive the gift of the Holy Spirit. *[Identity with God.]* And all those who believed were together and had all things in common (Acts 2:38, 44). *[Identity with God's people.]*

Jesus was baptized as an act of righteousness. He came to do His Father's will, not His own (John 6:38). He said and did what His Father told Him to do (John 12:49). Consequently, He maintained right relationships with both God and people.

If the perfect man, Jesus, submitted to baptism in order to fulfill righteousness, then we who are imperfect ought to do so also.

To change His lifestyle. John preached to people who believed in God and called for them to repent and be baptized. Baptism was referred to as a "baptism of repentance" (Mark 1:4; Luke 3:3). That means that repentance was the prerequisite of baptism. People were baptized as a visible sign to all that they had repented. As faith led to repentance, repentance led to baptism.

Our baptism today should also be a baptism of repentance. It is an outward visual aid of what has gone on inwardly— repentance—a change of direction—a difference in living. Jesus believed in God and He also repented. He did not repent of His own sin and guiltiness, for He had not sinned. But on the day of His baptism, He changed the way He would spend the rest of His life.

He left the security of His sheltered life at home and work at the carpenter's shop. He would now make the broader world His home and become God's prophet, priest, king, savior, redeemer, friend, physician, substitute, ransom, and shepherd for people. To submit to baptism is to acknowledge with a visual show-and-tell that we are willing to change some of our old life-styles in order to begin again.

Just how are faith, repentance, and baptism connected? In faith, we submit our minds to God. In repentance, we submit our wills to God. In baptism, we submit our physical bodies to God. Combined, we submit our total selves to God.

41

Jesus would do no less himself than He asks us to do.

To be identified. In His baptism, Jesus identified with the sins of humanity. Jesus was sinless. But sinlessness does not parade itself with an arrogant superiority complex. Real sinlessness humbles self to touch the sinfulness of man and says, "I understand. I am willing to be identified with you." Real sinlessness does not stand aloof, but comes close. That's what Jesus did in His baptism.

Jesus began His ministry by identifying with sinners in baptism. He concluded His earthly human ministry by identifying with sinners on the cross.

In a sense, His baptism was a visual pre-announcement that He would take man's sin into His body. He did it—on the cross! "And He Himself bore our sins in His body on the cross" (1 Peter 2:24).

His baptism was His entrance into a cross-carrying ministry. Since baptism is a symbol of a death and burial (Romans 6:3, 4), Jesus was giving a sneak preview that He would later identify with sinners by a voluntary death and burial in their stead, and that He would be raised again.

When we are baptized, we, too, identify ourselves with all sinners who need God's grace. To refuse baptism is to stand proudly on the bank as if we were not like those sinners. Someone has said that Hell is for people who think they are right, while Heaven is for people who admit they are not right and have done something about it.

If the perfect Jesus could identify with mankind, then surely we who are imperfect can do so also.

To be commissioned. John was emphasizing that the kingdom of God was at hand, but every kingdom needs a king. God publicly installed Jesus as the King when He declared, "This is my beloved Son, in whom I am well-pleased" (Matthew 3:17).

"This is my beloved Son" comes from Psalm 2, which was a royal Psalm that was used at the coronation of new kings. The Jews had expected the Messiah to be a king in fulfillment of the prophecy in Isaiah 9:6, 7.

> For a child will be born to us, a son will be given to us; And the government will rest on His shoulders; And His name will be called Wonderful Counselor, Mighty God, Eternal Father, Prince

of Peace. There will be no end to the increase of His government or of peace, on the throne of David and over His kingdom.

God would not disappoint the Jews in their expectation of a king. When He used that sentence so familiar at the coronation of Jewish kings, "This is my beloved Son," God was publicly coronating Jesus as the promised king.

But God added to the coronation sentence some unexpected words, "In whom I am well-pleased." Those words come from Isaiah 42:1, which is not a kingship passage at all. Rather, it begins a long suffering-servant passage that climaxed in Isaiah 53. This servant would bear our griefs, be pierced through for our transgressions, and be crushed for our iniquities.

By adding those words, God was declaring what kind of king Jesus would be. He would be a suffering-servant king. He would come to live among man, not just rule over them. He would take the wrongs of His subjects to himself. Their guilt would become His. What a King!

At His baptism, Jesus committed himself to the cross, putting the interests of others first and considering others worthy of His service, sacrifice, love, and forgiveness.

The earth had never had a king like that before and will never have another one like that again. Jesus was one-of-a-kind king. No wonder Paul said that He was the "only Sovereign, the King of kings and Lord of lords" (1 Timothy 6:15).

Jesus clearly understood the functional nature of His kingship. His first sermon at His hometown synagogue outlined the servant nature of it.

> The Spirit of the Lord is upon Me, because He anointed Me to preach the gospel to the poor. He has sent Me to proclaim release to the captives, and recovery of sight to the blind, to set free those who are downtrodden, to proclaim the favorable year of the Lord (Luke 4:18, 19).

Jesus didn't just *speak* about being a servant to people, He beautifully *lived* it out everyday in every way.

Does the fact that Jesus was commissioned to ministry at His baptism have anything to say about what happens when we are baptized? It surely does!

The early Christians understood baptism as both a commitment of the baptized and a commissioning of the baptized to service for the King. In fact, the second and third century Christians described baptism with the same term that was used for the military oath. When a person takes the military oath, he transfers from being a civilian to being in the troops. With the oath, he takes on both the privileges and the responsibilities of being on active duty.

At baptism, every Christian enters into active duty for the King. We enter into a real warfare with the devil and his tactics. But we don't enter into it defenseless. Our Commander in chief supplies us with His kind of armor,

Therefore, take up the full armor of God, that you may be able to resist in the evil day, and having done everything, to stand firm. Stand firm therefore, having girded your loins with truth, and having put on the breastplate of righteousness, and having shod your feet with the preparation of the gospel of peace; in addition to all, taking up the shield of faith with which you will be able to extinguish all the flaming missiles of the evil one. And take the helmet of salvation, and the sword of the Spirit, which is the word of God (Ephesians 6:13-17).

Fellowship is the "buddy system" in the army of God. Prayer is keeping in contact with the command post. Worship is honoring our commander in chief. Reading the Word is reading our "orders for the day."

The New Testament church was familiar with military terms that spotlighted the active duty status of the baptized—soldier (2 Timothy 2:3), be on the alert (1 Corinthians 16:13), armor (Ephesians 6:13), fight (1 Timothy 1:18), guard (Philippians 4:7), war (1 Peter 2:11), weapons, warfare, destruction of fortresses, and take captive (2 Corinthians 10:4, 5).

Early Christians knew that at baptism they changed sides. They had been transferred from allegiance to one king (Satan) to another king (Jesus). Early Christians took seriously their status as active-duty soldiers in God's army. The question is—do we?

Is it possible that some of us are not yet aware that we are in God's army and that there is a real battle going on? Have some of us stayed in the barracks while we let others do our fighting for us? Have some of us gone A.W.O.L. (away without official leave) immediately after our baptisms? Have some of us committed treason by deserting God's army to re-enlist in Satan's? Have some of us taken early retirement? Have some of us been involved long enough that we see ourselves as veterans who do not need to contribute to the battle any longer? Have some of us entered the battle without God's armor, got wounded, and decided never to face the enemy again? Have some of us become draft dodgers?

Have some of us hired substitutes to do our fighting for us? During the civil war in the United States, it was a common practice for a wealthy person to hire someone to take his place when drafted. Is that what we have done by hiring a preacher, missionary, youth minister, or other church staff member?

When Jesus was baptized, He was baptized *for us.* That doesn't mean that He was baptized in our place, but He was baptized for our benefit. He was baptized to enter into a ministry for us. When we are baptized, we, too, are to be baptized *for others.* We are to be baptized to enter into Christian service for the benefit of others. We are to follow Jesus, who followed-up His baptism by unselfish service. Jesus became a minister (servant) at His baptism, and so should we. The Master became a minister. What humility!

Sometimes a problem we have is that we ministers (and every Christian is a minister) act more like masters. What arrogance!

To receive power. How would Jesus convince people that He, a lowly carpenter, was the true king? At His baptism, Jesus received not only God's pronouncement, "This is My beloved Son," but also God's power for doing miracles, which Jesus used to authenticate His Messiah-ministry (Acts 2:22)—the Holy Spirit. The Spirit of God descended upon Jesus at His baptism. "Behold, the heavens were opened, and He saw the Spirit of God descending as a dove, and coming upon Him" (Matthew 3:16). Peter referred to this event when he said, "You know of Jesus of Nazareth, how God anointed Him with the Holy Spirit and with power" (Acts 10:38).

God also gives us the Holy Spirit.

"And Peter said to them, "Repent, and let each of you be baptized

45

in the name of Jesus Christ for the forgiveness of your sins; and you shall receive the gift of the Holy Spirit" (Acts 2:38).

It was after this that Jesus began His ministry. Immediately after recording the coming of the Holy Spirit and God's pronouncement, Luke wrote, "And when He began His ministry, Jesus Himself was about thirty years of age" (Luke 3:23).

But what kind of ministry would Jesus live out? He had power to move mountains. That's a bunch of power. How would He use it? How would you and I use that kind of power? Remember, He was still human and could cave in to human temptations to misuse that power.

Nowhere is a man's character tested more than by his use of great power (Holy Spirit) and status (King). Power can turn inward by using it for self-advantage, self-satisfaction, and self-service. Power turned inward can put down others, hurt them, neglect them, and make them feel inferior and second rate.

Immediately after recording that Jesus was anointed with the Holy Spirit and with power, Peter outlined Jesus' use of that power: "and how He went about doing good, and healing all who were oppressed by the devil; for God was with Him" (Acts 10:38).

However, the decision to use that power for doing good did not come without a battle. The battlelines were drawn—live for self or for others. That same battle is ours.

Indeed, Jesus was baptized with our benefit in mind. Would He follow it up with a life that had our benefit in mind? Would He resist the temptations to redirect His ministry? How would He use His power—for himself or for others? That is what we will look at next.

A Stick-to-it-ness

(Matthew 4:1-11)

Everyone Is Gifted

Every person is both gifted and gullible. We are gifted by God with certain abilities. God has gifted us with a purpose— that we use our gifts, abilities, and power to benefit others. "But to each one is given the manifestation of the Spirit for the common good" (1 Corinthians 12:7). "As each one has received a special gift, employ it is serving one another, as good stewards of the manifold grace of God" (1 Peter 4:10).

We are also gullible. We can be duped into using our gifts for our own good. The person who is gifted to make money may use it only to build bigger accounts for himself, like the farmer in Luke 12:18, 19:

> He said, "This is what I will do: I will tear down my barns and build larger ones, and there I will store all my grain and my goods. And I will say to my soul, 'Soul you have many goods laid up for many years to come; take your ease, eat, drink and be merry.'"

The person who is gifted with a beautiful singing voice may use it only to enhance self in the entertainment world while completely leaving out any ministry for God. The person who is gifted with motivating people may use that gift to become a master over people rather than inspiring people to become servants of God and of one another. The person with the power of charming people may use it to get whatever he wants out of people.

God gives us gifts with a purpose. The devil tempts us through our gifts with perversion. If we use our gifts with

47

perversion (selfishly), we become perverted people who will be miserable even though we are magnificently gifted. At no time are we tempted more severely than when we are being tested on how we are going to use our gifts. And no temptation has more potentially positive or negative results than that one.

Jesus possessed supernatural powers. The question was—how would He use that power. God, Jesus, and the devil knew that decision had to be made by Jesus himself. And that is the way it is with us. Each of us must wrestle with the temptation of the use of our lives. For whom will we live?

Jesus knew He had been commissioned to ministry. So he got off alone to decide once and for all how he would do that ministry. His decision was not whether or not He would do a ministry, but how. What would be His motives and methods? Would He do His ministry in a Jimmy Jones—Jonestown style or the self-giving style of a George Washington Carver? Would He be a getter or a giver? Would He reduce His standard of living and increase His standard of giving, or would He reduce His standard of giving to increase His standard of living? Would He adopt a cross kind of ministry or a crown kind of ministry? Would He seek honors or humility, status or service, crowds or disciples?

So Jesus got off by himself. Perhaps one of our difficulties is that we seldom slow down enough to be alone—to think, pray, ponder, meditate, and decide. We are rushaholics, workaholics, and goaholics. We all need to spend some time on our knees before we run on our feet. We need to get the accelerators of our lives off the floor boards and let our motors idle with the gears in neutral. If the devil doesn't make us too bad, he can make us too busy—too busy really to settle the important questions—for whom will I live, with what motives, purposes, and methods, and toward what end?

That is the testing that all of us experience. But sometimes we get so busy that we just go with the flow, and the rush of life has caught us up in a motive, method, and end that we did not really plan or intend. Sometimes we are like a small piece of wood being carried about in the torrents of a fast stream. That is sad! That is to lose control of self! And it is to become more captives to what is pushing and shoving us than to be the captains of our destiny! I wonder whether that's not what happened to the Howard Hughes and Elvis Presleys of our time. It has happened to me.

God wants each of us to slow down enough to take stock of our abilities, gifts, opportunities, directions, and powers and to commit ourselves to a life that squares with His will. But that decision must be ours and no one else's. God will try to influence us one way and the devil will try to influence us another. But we must decide. God had already influenced Jesus by announcing at His baptism that Jesus was to be a suffering, servant, self giving kind of King. Then it became the devil's turn to try to influence Him.

Jesus' Temptation

So Jesus faced temptations of the devil. It is not evil to be tempted. To be tempted is to be tested. From God's perspective, it is for our good. For in the midst of this kind of testing, we can settle the direction we want our lives to go. Testing is designed to help us overcome sin, not cave-in to it. It is meant to solidify us, not soften us. It is meant to strengthen us, not weaken us. It is meant to help us master life, not be mastered by it. It is meant to mold us, not destroy us. It is meant to help us stand up with purpose, not knock us down with perversion. It is meant to unify us with God's direction, not separate us from Him.

But the devil would like something else to happen when we are tested. He would like to see us cave in, weaken, soften, be mastered, destroyed, knocked down, and separated from God. He wants the tests to detour us from God's life of unselfishness. He desires to see the tests cause us to turn inward rather than upward and outward.

To say it another way—Jesus was on track. And God wanted the tests to help Jesus himself decide to stay on track no matter what. But the devil wanted Jesus to use the tests to throw a switch and change tracks. Tests can either minister to us or mess us up; delight us or detour us; make us or break us. It is strictly up to us—no one else. Each of us must decide for himself. God has gifted us, but He will not decide what we do with those gifts. He leaves that up to us. That is part of the glory that goes along with being a human. It is an awesome responsibility. Will we allow ourselves to be used by God or not? That's what the tests that challenge our decision about the use or abuse of our abilities is all about. And no person can bypass making that decision. We will consciously make that decision and commit ourselves to a life style or we will go with the flow. That itself is a decision and a commitment.

The first temptation: "If you are the Son of God, command that these stones become bread" (Matthew 4:3). At first it may sound as if the devil is doubting Jesus' Sonship, "If," he says, and he wants Jesus to prove it. But that is not the case at all. Satan knew Jesus well. There are four different ways an "if" clause is written in the Greek, each of which has a different connotation. The "if" clauses here are written in the Greek to affirm the reality of something, not to question it. In English we might say, "Since you are the Son of God," or "Because you are the Son of God. . . ."

In each of these temptations, Satan's first attempt is to try to get Jesus to take advantage of His privileged status. The same test comes to any person who reaches any plateau of leadership. "Since you are the preacher, pastor, elder, deacon, committee chairman, trustee, a member of the board of directors, president of a Christian group or institution, why stick to the rules everybody else goes by? You are special; so take advantage of it. Throw your weight around some. Let people know right away where the power lies. Surely you don't have to stay within the traditional boundary lines. Although John wrote that Jesus came to dwell *among* us (John 1:14), the devil tempted Jesus at the beginning of His ministry to dwell *above* the people by saying, "*Since* you are the Son of God. . . ." Whatever else Satan would say, he wanted Jesus to consider doing it out of Jesus' special status. "Go ahead, Jesus, you are the Son of God. You have the right to do it."

The first temptation was not only an attempt to motivate Jesus to take advantage of His status, but also to enter into His ministry thinking of himself first.

Jesus had spent forty days fasting in the wilderness, and He was hungry. So Satan's first temptation centered on a basic, non-sinful desire of Jesus—the desire for food, "Command that these stones become bread." At Jesus feet would have been tens of thousands of little round stones that resembled mini loaves of bread. It would have been easy for Jesus to have converted the stones into bread. And why not? After all, how could He possibly minister to people if He would not take care of himself? Satan was advocating the philosophy of "Look out for number one" and "Pull your own strings."

What would be wrong with eating some bread after a forty-day fast? Nothing! But that is not the real issue here. The real issue is whether or not Jesus would begin using His special gifts and powers for His own advantage. Everyone of us will be tempted to use our gifts for ourselves. But will we use them *only* for ourselves?

I think there is another angle to this first temptation, one that is of paramount significance. It has to do with the *methods* Jesus would use to get a following. Jesus knew well how the heavy Roman taxes had kept the poor people so impoverished that they could hardly keep bread on the table. That pathetic situation touched Jesus. He really cared about the hunger of men. He told parables about it (Luke 16:19-31). He made it clear that God would consider how we did or did not provide for the hungry as a criterion at the last Judgement (Matthew 25:35, 42).

So Satan tested Jesus at one of His most tender spots—the opportunity to help people by turning stone into bread. If He could do it for himself, He could do it for others. And what a way to get an immediate massive following. Who wouldn't follow someone who would convert the rocks in your front yard into loaves of *Wonder Bread?*

And after all, didn't God give His people manna in the wilderness? So what would be wrong with this? Nothing, unless it is the dominant characteristic of His ministry. Then it would lure men to follow Him for selfish reasons—what they could get out of it for themselves. It would turn His disciples into go-getters instead of go-givers. It would also bypass the real needs of humanity. People, not pebbles, needed to be changed. They needed love in their lives, not loaves in their stomachs. Jesus knew that souls needed to become brothers, not stones become bread, if the world would really be benefited. Jesus knew that too much hunger was caused by selfishness, greed, hatred, evil, and laziness. Hearts, not hearths, needed to be changed. The way to do that was the cross; so Jesus was not about to trade the cross for a bakery shop. He was not going to trade in nails in His hands for bread in them.

Jesus also knew that people who followed Him just to get bread would not stay with Him long. Later He did feed thousands. The next day they came back for another handout, but they deserted Jesus when He taught them about their relationship with God (John 6).

Jesus also had history on His side. Old Israel was fed by God in the wilderness, but they lived a life of complaining. Israel had caved in to "loving" God for the material things. So Jesus quoted to the devil what Moses had said to old Israel, "Man shall not live on bread alone, but on every word that proceeds out of the mouth of God" (Matthew 4:4; Deuteronomy 8:3). Jesus did not want to begin His ministry by dangling material advantages before people as their motivation for following Him.

This temptation is still around today in different forms. There is the wealth fad being taught by several "spiritual" hucksters. They teach that God wants everyone rich. So if you send them your money, God will honor that by materially blessing you. Such teaching smacks of a spiritual Las Vegas ring—put your money in so you can strike it rich by getting more money out. That is ridiculous teaching. God is the God of both the rich and the poor (Proverbs 22:2), and He loves both. One of the prayers we should pray is to make us neither rich nor poor (Proverbs 30:8, 9). The Biblical purpose for having riches is not necessarily to *get* more, but to *give* more (Ephesians 4:28; 1 Timothy 6:17-19). Lack of riches has nothing to with lack of spirituality. Both Jesus and Paul were poor.

In denying this temptation, Jesus taught us that God does not call the church to get a following by promising profit. Nor does God call us to a life of self-preservation, but rather self-sacrifice. Jesus did not use His power to save himself at the beginning of His ministry, nor did He seek to preserve himself at the end of His ministry. He stayed in the wilderness hungering, and He stayed on the cross dying.

The second temptation. Again Satan appealed to Jesus' special status, "Since you are the Son of God." If that didn't work the first time, perhaps it would the second time. We may resist taking advantage of our privileged position once, but the real test is whether or not we will resist time and time again.

Satan knew of Jesus' great power, and he suggested that

Jesus use those powers to become an instant sensation and gain an instant great following. "Then the devil took Him into the holy city; and he stood Him on the pinnacle of the temple" (Matthew 4:5). Satan's second temptation hit Jesus at another tender spot. Jesus certainly wanted people to believe in the power of God, and this method would do it.

The Evil Knievels always draw a crowd. Imagine how the people would have flocked to Jesus if He would have jumped off the pinnacle of the temple into the valley 450 feet below, or into the midst of the temple in the middle of the masses, and just before hitting the ground would have come to a slow stop—without even using a parachute. How spectacular! That would be even better than trying to jump over the Grand Canyon on a motorcycle. Yes, Jesus could have gained quite a following by heeding Satan's suggestion. After all, He *was* the Son of God. God would surely be with Him; so why not jump?

There are some problems with using sensationalism to gain a following. *First,* it calls for us to test God by *demanding* that He prove we can trust Him by some sensational demonstration. *Second,* it lures shallow people to instant belief. *Third,* it replaces God's means of developing faith, for faith comes by hearing the Word of God (Romans 10:17). Jesus would not replace sentences with sensationalism. *Fourth,* a faith that is based upon sensationalism only is rootless and won't last. In the story of the rich man and Lazarus, the rich man wanted God to send someone from the dead to talk to people, ". . . but if someone goes to them from the dead, they will repent" (Luke 16:30). To that request came the clear reply, "If they do not listen to Moses and the prophets, neither will they be persuaded if someone rises from the dead" (Luke 16:31). Faith that rests totally upon sight is not really faith. Our convictions must come from a deeper source than just the eyes.

In fact, Jesus does not trust himself to those whose faith is based upon only eyesight, "Now when He was in Jerusalem at the Passover, during the feast, many believed in His name, beholding His signs which He was doing. But Jesus, on His part, was not entrusting Himself to them, for He knew all men" (John 2:23, 24).

Jesus knew that old Israel in the wilderness had observed miracle after miracle but didn't maintain a long-range faith in

God. He also knew that the cities in which He did most of His miracles did not believe in Him (Matthew 11:20).

Of course, we must believe that nothing is impossible with God. He is still the powerful, surprising God of miracles. But not to believe in Him unless we see miracles is to have shallow faith.

Fifth, to attract people by sensationalism calls for a follow-up of more spectacular sensations. That method for enlisting a crowd calls for a continual game plan of outdoing the previous sensations. *Sixth*, sensationalism is not the way to use God's power. God does not want us to draw people to ourselves by showing them how much we can do with God's gifts. We are not to use God's powers to enhance ourselves.

The temptation to draw a following with the sensational is still around today. Some churches specialize in offering the greatest show in town, the best miracle going, or the finest contest ever dreamed up. Of course, a more spectacular show, a more stupendous miracle, and a more exciting contest has to be created for the following year. And the attention of the people becomes fixed on the show, miracle, and/or contest instead of on Jesus. If people are motivated to give to the sensational, then something more sensational has to come to keep the giving up. Just wait. The next letter or announcement will be more appealing than the one before.

Seventh, this temptation was one of the ones old Israel caved in on. They were constantly demanding that God do something more spectacular to reassure them that He was God. God got tired of the littleness of their faith—or, really, their lack of faith. Jesus was not going to enter His ministry, nor conduct His ministry, demanding that God prove himself by passing the sensation test that Jesus would write. While old Israel demanded a continual display of the extraordinary, Jesus would not. So He quoted to Satan the words Moses said to old Israel in the wilderness, "You shall not put the Lord your God to the test" (Matthew 4:7; Deuteronomy 6:16).

The third temptation. Satan went all out this time and offered Jesus the whole world on a platter.

Again, the devil took Him to a very high mountain, and showed Him all the kingdoms of the world, and their glory; and

54

he said to Him, "All these things will I give You, if You fall down and worship me" (Matthew 4:8, 9).

Satan went after another tender spot of Jesus, for Jesus wanted the whole world to be His, and thus God's. He had come to be King, and in this temptation He had instant kingship of the whole world offered to Him. After all, Satan was the ruler of this world (John 12:31; 14:30; 16:11), and he was ready to turn it over to Jesus on *Satan's* terms. Could Satan have given this temporary earthly world to Jesus? Of course he could, for he has been giving bits and pieces of it to those who bow down and follow him ever since Jesus refused to take it all on Satan's terms.

Satan was trying to get Jesus to adopt a ministry of expediency and compromise. Expediency was possible because Jesus could get the world out from under the tyranny of Rome. However, compromise was the method: "Fall down and worship me." If Jesus had done that, He would have had the world bowing at His feet, but it would have been an unchanged world, and a condemned world.

Yielding to the temptation of expediency and compromise was part of old Israel's problem. They wanted to get things done on their own time table. They wanted things to happen—immediately. Remember their impatience with Moses, and how they manufactured their own god to worship? Jesus wasn't about to follow their mistake; so He quoted to the devil what Moses had said to old Israel, "You shall worship the Lord your God, and serve Him only" (Matthew 4:10; Deuteronomy 6:13).

This temptation is still around today. It is seen when the church is tempted to get things accomplished fast—such a fast growth—at the expense of compromise. It is seen in drawing the world by becoming like the world. We have been duped today into thinking that we must be right if the world comes flocking to us. But we must learn that not everything that grows fast is necessarily good. Cancer grows, and sometimes very rapidly.

We are to win the world—but on God's terms (Matthew 28:19, 20).

Conclusion. Jesus decided not to get a crowd by economically bribing them, wowing them with sensationalism, or compromising. He would not allow Satan to win by offering Him rewards without responsibilities, security without service, success without sacrifice, followers without faith. Jesus refused to be lured or tricked.

Only one doorway for effective ministry remained open to Jesus—that of lowly, tiring, costly service that would eventually lead to the cross.

Jesus taught us by His reactions to these temptations that the end—crowds, followers, the world—does not justify the means. To stick with God's plan, way, and methods is absolutely essential.

From Jesus' temptation experiences, we can learn that we are to face temptations rather than shy away from them. We should look at them as spiritual exercises designed by God to get us into shape and to keep us in shape.

I am reminded of my football career. As a freshman in high school, I decided I wanted to be a pro football star. I was so enthusiastic and excited that first day of practice. I gloried in catching passes and running around would-be tacklers. I felt I was a great success already.

But then the coach told us to lie down. For the next forty-five minutes, we did push-ups, scissors kicks, sit-ups, and other types of strenuous exercises.

My football career both began and ended on that first day. I failed to see that those exercises had anything to do with winning games. They were inconvenient, painful, and tough. I wanted to play, not work; so I took off my uniform and never returned. I let the stress test flunk me.

But Jesus faced up to the tests and won the victory by refusing to give in to His personal wishes. He didn't give up God's goals and values. He would not be moved to go Satan's way. In a sense, Jesus began His ministry declaring, "Not my will, the crowd's will, or Satan's will, but God's will be done." And Jesus maintained that commitment to the cross.

We too can gain the victory by sticking to God's methods, purposes, and goals by using our God-given powers and gifts for service to others, not for enhancing status for self.

Fasting

It is easy to overlook Jesus' fast in this temptation experience. Why did Jesus fast? Not to do a favor to God in hopes that God would return a favor to Jesus; not to save money on His food bill to send the savings to a mission field; not to disfigure His countenance so He would look like a living sacrifice; not to have something to brag about. All of the above are reasons some people fast today.

People fasted in Bible days to heighten their dependency upon God. In a fast, God's people offered themselves as vessels for God to fill and use. While eating tends to focus attention on oneself, a fast can free us up to put our attention on God and His unselfish ministry. God asked people to fast as a means of heightening their attention to God and their sensitivity to His way. A fast was to help man covenant himself to God's kind of ministry. So a fast is not a selfish ritual, but an unselfish preparation for making unselfish commitments.

> Is this not the fast which I chose, to loosen the bonds of wickedness, to undo the bands of the yoke, and to let the oppressed go free, and break every yoke? Is it not to divide your bread with the hungry and bring the homeless poor into the house; when you see the naked, to cover him; and not to hide yourself from you own flesh? Then your light will break out like the dawn, and your recovery will speedily spring forth; and your righteousness will go before you; the glory of the Lord will be your rear guard. Then you will call, and the Lord will answer; you will cry, and He will say, "Here I am." If you remove the yoke from your midst, the pointing of the finger, and speaking wickedness, and if you give yourself to the hungry, and satisfy the desire of the afflicted, then your light will rise in darkness, and your gloom will become like midday. And the Lord will continually guide you, and satisfy your desire in scorched places, and give strength to your bones; and you will be like a watered garden and like a spring of water whose waters do not fail. And those from among you will rebuild the ancient ruins; you will raise up the age-old foundations; and you will be called the repairer of the breach, the restorer of the streets in which to dwell (Isaiah 58:6-12).

So it is not unusual that Jesus fasted while considering His role in a ministry of caring for people. Jesus rejected the devil's attempts to lure Him onto a pathway that could bypass humble service. Jesus probably settled His commitment while fasting, and simply verbalized it with the tests hurled at Him.

In the fast, Jesus felt His commitment and thought it through. In the test, He solidified that commitment at the yes-and-no level. After this wilderness experience, He practiced His commitment. He consistently refused to let anyone or anything detour Him from His priority.

And what priority was that? It was the cross—the denial of himself for the betterment of others.

6

by Knofel Staton

Leaving, Following, and Fulfillment

(Matthew 4:18-22)

For a moment, think about your community. Is there a section in it that needs a major moral overhaul? If not, then think about a neighboring city. Got one in mind? Now how would you go about changing it? Want to tackle it single-handedly? Would you want some other people to help you?

Whom would you want to help you? How about an oddball hermit who lives alone way out in the boondocks? When he does come to town, he is surely noticed because his clothing makes him look more like an animal than a person. How about a tyrant who is very narrowly prejudiced against most people and is known to lead his own violent holocaust to get rid of those different people? How about a timid biracial person who gets physically sick? How about two brothers who are so accustomed to getting their way that when they don't, they go into instant explosion? How about two other brothers who are as different as cotton candy and acid? One brother sort of melts into the woodwork. You hardly know he is around. But when you do notice him, he is considerate, kind, and compatible. But the other brother stands out like a lone infant crying in a church service. He is a headstrong, arrogant braggart; a know-it-all who often thinks he knows more than anyone about everything.

Who wants a supportive group like that surrounding him? Jesus does. Because Jesus doesn't see us just the way we once were and lock us into that perspective for the rest of our lives.

Jesus is the same yesterday, today, and forever, but He knows that we are not! We are constantly changing. So Jesus

59

looks beyond what we are today and sees our potential. He then taps into that potential to free us to become what we can become. That's part of what He meant when He said, "I came that they may have life, and might have it abundantly" (John 10:10).

We have too much of a tendency to hold ourselves down when God wants to let us go. We often imprison ourselves to our own constructed cells with thick walls and sturdy bars. Those walls and bars are made of the material of past experiences, present environments, and our own self images. We look at that trinity and think we are trapped forever. The door to the cell is locked and someone "out there" has the key, but he won't open the door.

That's mere fantasy. Jesus has given us the key. We've locked the door on the inside. No one else has locked it. And He is our companion urging us, inspiring us, equipping us, and waiting for us to unlock that door from the inside and enjoy who we are, what we are, and the potential that He has given to us.

Once upon a time, many eggs were delivered to a farm. When the eggs matured, a new flock of infant geese was hatched. But one little creature was not like the others. His beak was longer and more crooked. His wings were proportionally larger. He didn't have the beautiful toned color of his fellow geese. His feet were malformed. The webbed feet did not form on his legs; so he could not handle being in the water as the other geese. He just couldn't get swimming down. While the other geese floated so graciously, he sank. Because his legs and feet were deformed, he couldn't run across the lot with the cute swing and sway of the other geese. He was a freak. The other geese made fun of him.

One day, way up in the sky, a large bird saw the flock of healthy geese on the ground and zeroed in on them. With wings stretched out, he swiftly zoomed out of the sky like a jet. As he got closer and closer, the deformed, freakish goose watched with intense interest. He began to recognize something familiar. As that bird got dangerously close, that goose realized that he was not a goose at all. He was born an eagle just like that eagle in the sky. And so he opened his wings and soared into the sky with his new-found eagle friend. He finally got a glimpse of his potential and began to tap into it.

We are too much like that "deformed, freakish 'goose.'" We have spent too much time seeing our potential from the perspective of the people around us.

It is time to look up and see the "eagle," Jesus, who came to give us a glimpse of what we really are—people made in the image of God. Jesus freely demonstrated what it really means to be a human. And He said, "Follow me." Don't follow the philosophies springing up. Don't follow a psychology or sociology textbook. Follow Jesus if you want to know life that has potential to escape from a locked cage.

When Jesus was here, He specialized in helping people unlock their cages. That oddball hermit was John the Baptist. The narrowly prejudiced person who led in a temporary holocaust was the apostle Paul. The timid, sickly person was Timothy. The two brothers accustomed to instant explosions were James and John. The two opposite brothers, one who sat down and stood back and one who stood up and stood out, were Andrew and Peter.

These men unlocked their cells and really soared.

The Invitation

Jesus invited Peter, Andrew, James, and John to unlock their cells when He said, "Follow me, and I will make you fishers of men." There are many interesting dimensions to that invitation.

He promised no immediate rewards. He wasn't after people who were going to follow just for what they would get out of it for themselves. There was none of this "pull your own strings," "look out for number one" coming out of Jesus. Jesus knew that such thinking merely reduces the size of our cages.

He promised His companionship. He did not ask them to go it alone. He would be with them. He would not be with them as a dictating general spouting orders, but as a model who would be and do what He would call them to be and do. He did not say, "Follow my *orders.*" He said, "Follow *Me.*" Jesus does have commands, but we aren't going to learn much from His commands if we bypass Him as a person.

He promised a purpose bigger than those men. We do people a terrible injustice by not challenging them beyond their present "prison cells." People need meaningful purpose for living. Jesus does us a favor by calling us to meaningful responsibilities. Some of the keenest pyschologists, such as Eric Erikson and Gordon Allport, today are teaching that one of the distinctive characteristics of human nature is that we humans do not really mature until we have a definite objective—a goal bigger than our self-centered interests in which we lose ourselves for the well-being of others.

That's what Jesus did with those fishermen. When He said, "I will make you fishers of men," He was not suggesting that they totally had to abandon their fishing nets. However, He knew that they realized that life is more than making a living. An occupation for income is needed, but life is not satisfying if it is not coupled with something bigger than a money-making job.

So Jesus offered them bigger nets in a wider sea. He offered them a catch that would bring fellowship, not just fish; a filled purpose, not just a filled purse; and a life, not just a livelihood. He offered them a life that would relate to people, not just to things; that could make a difference in the world long after they would die; that could cause people to thank them (neither fish nor things can ever thank us); that could affect individuals, families, employer-employee relationships, and communities; that could tap potentials they had never used; that could make them eagles.

Jesus has never changed that invitation. He does not call any of us to just a life of salvation with a promised mansion in Heaven. That is ours, but life is more than lying around on a spiritual beach of comfort allowing the sound of the waves to lure us to sleep and the spiritual rays of His Word to give us that super-healthy-tan look. We are in the world on purpose—with a purpose.

We may have different ways to make money. That's our *occupation*. The world needs thousands of different occupations. Our occupations should relate to our temporary interest, abilities, and aptitudes—truck driving, farming, business management, medicine, store sales, and teaching. But every Christian is called to have the same *vocation* (purpose, calling, mission). That vocation-mission-purpose is to bring human beings into reconciliation with God through Jesus. God calls us all to be His functioning ambassadors. We are to link that mission to our occupations (be open to opportunities to introduce people to God). We are also to link that purpose to our families (use family opportunities to introduce friends to God's life-style). We are also to link that calling to a local congregation. Global missions is only possible to the extent that Christians root themselves in a local body of believers. For it is only in the local congregations that community relatedness, accountability, nurturing, resources, encouragement, support, prayers, discipline, education, modeling, counseling, unconditional love, and continuity of fellowship are possible. And these combined factors are essential for living out our mission for Christ.

Since all Christians have been called to the same vocation, then we are to stand together with equal honor and dignity, in spite of the way we earn money to sustain our lives. Our different occupations may give us different plateaus of status in the world, but our same purpose puts us on the same ground in the church.

The People Invited

Just what kinds of people does Jesus invite to be His disciples? This is what you're going to like!

Average people. These four men came from Main Street, not Wall Street. They had ego problems, they would quarrel, they backed away when they were scared at the crucifixion, and they often asked questions that showed lack of understanding. They were not superstars until years later.

Below-average people. Jesus even uses some of the most unlikely people to be His disciples. He used Mark, a quitter, and Timothy—that timid guy.

Extraordinary people. Jesus is no respecter of persons. He calls those who have excelled in their occupations—Matthew, Paul, and Zaccheus.

Busy people. Notice that Jesus called men while they were already busy. Jesus isn't looking for someone who needs something to fill up his time.

Inexperienced people. None of these had been fishers of men before. In this activity, they were babes—novices. Several times, Jesus called them little children. Some people do not live out their purpose because they've never done it before. We think introducing people to God is for the experts. Nope! It's for people like fishermen, who have never done it before, but who are willing to learn and to try.

Followers. "Follow me" is the command issued to people who know how to follow. Everyone of us is a follower. No person can exist without being a follower of other people, ideals, or instincts. No one can be a good fisher of fish who has not followed the advice of other fishermen of the signs of the weather, of the tides, and of other tricks of the trade.

Flexible people. Each one of these men was open to change, and each did change. They were not committed to come "Just as I Am" and then to stay "Just as I Am." James and John, whom Jesus nicknamed "Sons of thunder," became mellow. Peter gave up His arrogant know-it-all attitudes. Andrew came out of obscurity and according to history evangelized in Southern Russia—and was crucified for doing so. God does not call any of us because He is so tickled with our dispositions that He never wants us to change. Is it possible that too many people remain basically unchanged? Do they bring into the church their secular dispositions and remain committed to keep that alive and "well" until Jesus returns?

Courageous people. Sure, these men got scared at times. But they stuck with Jesus even though doing so made them sail against the social winds of their day. They were criticized, questioned, ridiculed, misunderstood—and eventually killed.

Persistent people. A fisherman who brings in his net too soon will catch little. There is the need to wait with patience—to discourage our discouragement and to procrastinate our procrastinations.

Duty-bound people. The men Jesus called did not do things just because doing so was fun. Professional fishing is tough. And there is much about it that is drudgery, not delight. When Jesus called these four, all four were doing drudgery tasks out of a sense of duty. Neither casting nets nor mending nets gets a high mark on the fun-scale. Neither gives one a tingling, thrilling sensation that he is doing something fulfilling to the soul.

Jesus calls people to live above the "I'll do it if it gives me a tingle" philosophy. Serving God is indeed delightful, but not everything about it is fun. Some of it is sheer drudgery, but it is necessary. God needs people who will do things for no other reason than it is necessary to do.

Do you know what I hate about writing a book? The actual writing of it. Writing is not fun. Neither is getting out of bed in the morning, shaving, driving on the freeway, answering mail, paying bills, filling the car at a self-service gas station in the rain, changing a flat tire, or a thousand other things that we do out of duty. God needs people who will get up and get out and get going because they are committed.

Individualistic people. No two people are alike, and God does not expect us to be. No one has ever been exactly like you, and no one ever will. God does not expect you to check in your own personal identification marks to follow Jesus. We do not file off our fingerprints and eliminate our faces so we can come to Jesus as neutral, unidentifiable persons. Nor do we graft on to our fingertips the prints of another human so God has identical twins coming to Him.

All of us are to progress toward becoming like Jesus in character, but we will still be different from each other. We are biologically different. We each have a different biological genetic coding. We are socially different. No two people have had identical environments, for each has a brother or sister that the other does not have. We are psychologically different. We each have our own personality. God does not eliminate that. Instead, He channels it and uses it. At the same time, He wants us to change whatever needs to be changed to be more Christlike in our attitudes and activities.

We can easily see how God uses differences by considering these first four disciples he called.

Andrew. Andrew must have had a well-rounded, agreeable personality that gave him instant rapport with people. Every time we see him, he is a people-accepting person. He was one of the four who attended the wedding feast with Jesus. Andrew wasn't too busy to share in somebody's joy. He was the one who had established such a trust with a little lad that he knew about his lunch and encouraged him to share it. How did Andrew know about that lunch? The answer probably lies in how Andrew spent time with people. He didn't just touch and go. He talked; he listened; he got to know what was going on in their lives.

Andrew was the one disciple that other disciples brought people to so they could meet Jesus (John 12:20-22). He must have been an instant breaker of barriers that stood between people.

He seemed to have no relational problems. He even

brought his brother, Peter, to Jesus (John 1:40, 41). Many times brothers and sisters do not get along that well. But evidently Andrew and Peter were friends as well as brothers. Andrew's unassuming, gracious, and caring nature was a buffer that prevented his brother's hardheaded nature from negatively affecting him. Andrew evidently carried no prejudices against small lads, Greeks, or members of his family.

There is a real need for "Andrews" today—those people who break down barriers, who are not threatened, with whom people feel comfortable, and who care more about people than praise.

Peter. Now Peter was different—*really* different from Andrew. While Andrew was backstage, Peter was often on center stage, drawing attention to himself. Jesus gave him the nickname Peter, which means little rock. Peter was really hard-headed. Several times he put his mouth into high gear while his mind was still in neutral. He tried to correct Jesus and criticize Him (Mark 8:31, 32; Luke 8:43-45). He would brag about his big plans, "Even though all may fall away . . . I will not deny You" (Matthew 26:33-35).

But Peter changed. He once heard Jesus say that even the Messiah doesn't know everything (Matthew 24:36). That had to impress this man. Later in Jerusalem, at a major conference, Peter listened first and spoke later (Acts 15:7ff). He learned how to respond to challenges with carefully selected words (Acts 4:8-12). While he had a tough time giving forgiveness in his early years (Matthew 18:21), he later preached forgiveness. He laid aside his Jewish prejudices to evangelize and eat with non-Jews. Instead of putting himself in the spotlight, he caused people to turn their eyes upon Jesus. Jesus was the center of his message. He was so good at lifting up Jesus that, according to tradition, he was finally crucified upside down.

James and John. These two men were pills. Jesus himself nicknamed them sons of thunder. They must have grown up together as a temper-tantrum team getting their way all the time. On one occasion, they tried to persuade Jesus to destroy a village because someone there hurt their feelings (Luke 9:51-54). They tried to manipulate their way to the top slots in Jesus' kingdom (Matthew 20:22-27). They tried to cut people off who didn't do things their way (Luke 9:49).

But God channeled those boys. James was the first apostle to be killed because of his faith—and he didn't try to fight back. John wrote more about love than any other New Testament writer. The sons of thunder became models of tenderness. Their attitudes changed, but they kept their individualities.

Conclusion

The calling of these four (and later others) teaches us many truths:

1. Our individual differences can make a difference for God. It is in the symphony of our differences playing the same vocational tune of God's mission that the world can best hear the music of God's good news.

2. Because God's world is varied, He needs our variety. One person, because of his individuality, can draw some people to God that other kinds of people cannot.

3. We will never be used by God to draw people with our own individuality unless we are willing to start.

4. There comes a time to lay down our nets and pick up His.

5. We have the same vocation for missions while carrying out different occupations for money.

6. Christianity is not a one-man show.

7. Church work is to be a shared ministry.

8. We disciple others best when modeling the Christian life by spending time with people.

9. No one is to stay the way he has been or is now. We are to be becoming more Christlike.

10. We can reach our potential only as we give ourselves to a purpose bigger than ourselves—God's purpose.

Jesus has never changed His invitation: "Follow me, and I will make you fishers of men." It is not an invitation to become a lone-ranger workaholic but a functioning partner who depends upon Jesus first. He wants us in the yoke *with Him*. "Take My yoke upon you, and learn from me, for I am gentle and humble in heart; and you shall find rest for your souls. For My yoke is easy, and My load is light" (Matthew 11:29, 30). Do *easy* and *light* mean that He calls us just to skate through life? No! Not at all! His yoke demands earnest effort.

Easy means well-fitted. His yoke is tailor-made for our individualities; so the load does not add friction to us. The responsibility may seem heavy, but with Him it is light. He makes it that way. What a yokefellow He is.

Those four men began reaching their potential, feeling their joy, becoming content with living, and being filled to the brim with a sense of fulfillment when out of trust in Jesus they "immediately left the nets, . . . the boat and their father, and followed Him" (Matthew 4:20, 22).

Do you have any "nets" and "boats" that are keeping you from following Jesus? Do you have any people you are so attached to that you are not free to follow another person—Jesus? Those men left their nets and boats, but they would eventually gain the whole world.

James and John left their father temporarily but would keep him eternally, while inheriting a host of other family members—God's total family.

How about you? Are you ready—really—to do some leaving and some following?

Floating or Sinking?

(Matthew 5-7)

Kamala and Amala were eight and one-half years old when they were discovered. But they had to be dealt with as infants. Neither the boy nor the girl had any language, and their behavioral characteristics were totally those of an animal. Although they were born as humans and looked human, they acted like animals.

No one knows the details, but evidently their parents were killed when these two were babies. The children were thrown into a pack of wolves, which nurtured them and modeled life for them. Consequently, when they were discovered, they ran on all fours with the wolves and made only wolf-like sounds (*Sociology: A Book of Readings*, Koenig, Hopper, and Gross; Prentice Hall, 1953, pp. 82-85).

Several years ago, the news broke about a "chicken boy" found on the East coast. Neighbors began to have suspicions, and so they called the authorities. They found him in the hen house. Although a teenager, he made only chicken-like sounds and ate with the chickens in a chicken-like manner. From his birth, he was taken to the hen house and had since spent his whole life with the chickens.

Not one of these three people developed certain human characteristics, but acquired, in their place, the characteristics modeled before them in the environments in which they interacted.

Without having our created nature modeled before us, we will not develop certain characteristics that God has given us as humans created in His image and likeness.

69

So Jesus couldn't say, "Follow Me," and then distance himself from those followers. That would be like saying to a newborn baby, "Now act like a human," and then turning that baby over to the wolves or chickens.

God has told us that as a person thinks, so he is (Proverbs 23:7). The direction of our thinking comes from the environment in which we interact.

Jesus knew that our activities come from the way we think; so He taught in a way that could reshape our thought patterns and thus redirect our behavioral practices. He wants His followers to begin to think as He thinks and, out of that, to begin to live the way He lives.

Jesus did not just model His behavior, He also opened the door to His inner self so we could see the inner attitudes that shaped His activities. It is one thing to observe someone act in certain ways, but it is another thing to know why—from the inside out! If we do not know what is happening on the inside, we may copy another's outer actions without having the inner reasons. But Jesus does not want us to do that with Him. He wants us to see His inner attitudes so we will let those grow inside of us. Then our actions that square with His won't be just copycat pretending.

Beautiful Attitudes

Jesus began the Sermon on the Mount with a discussion of many of those beautiful attitudes that provided the inner thrust of His outer life.

But before we look at those attitudes, we need to consider the meaning of the word *blessed* that Jesus links to each of these attitudes.

Blessed: *Blessed* means happy, but it isn't the instant happiness that is triggered by what is going on around us. Did you ever wake up in the morning "happy" about a planned outing, and then the "happiness" washed away when the sky clouded over and it started raining? That is not a blessed kind of happiness. Jesus' blessed kind of happiness doesn't flatten when its balloon gets pricked. It doesn't sink when the flood waters rise. The blessed person is the buoyed-up person. He keeps afloat. He doesn't cave in.

He may live amidst suffering; people may hate him; people may slander him; he may face death. But through it all, he can be called blessed. In fact, the word *blessed* is used with all the above circumstances (James 5:11; 1 Peter 3:14; Luke 6:22; 1 Peter 4:14; Revelation 14:13). A good understanding of *blessed* is *buoyed up*. What buoys us up is not what is on the outside pressing in on us, but what is on the inside propelling us. Ella Wilcox has put it this way.

> One ship drives east and another drives west
> With the selfsame winds that blow.
> 'Tis the set of the sails
> And not the gales
> Which tells us the way to go.

("The Winds of Fate," *Masterpieces of Religious Verse*, Harper/Row, 1948, p. 314.)

It is the same with us. It is the set of our inner selves and not the storms raging outside that directs which way we go. Will we sink or float? Because He wants us to float, Jesus shares some of those inner attitudes that can buoy us up.

Humility (Poor in Spirit): Being "poor in Spirit" does not mean being a poor-spirited person, but rather a person who realizes that he doesn't have his spiritual life all together. Thus, he is in need—in need of *learning more* and in need of *leaning more* upon God and upon God's people. The poor in spirit admits, "I do not have all the answers. I must turn to God's guidance and follow His way." Thus, he is not *in*dependent, but *inter*dependent. Few things set us up to fall faster than an arrogance that tells us we have already arrived. The arrogant person feels he needs neither God nor others. Jesus was not that way. We see that in His dependence upon God, His prayer life, and His fellowship with others.

No wonder the kingdom of Heaven is promised to the poor in spirit. For only the humble are open to receive God's rulership.

Are you poor in spirit? Do you admit your weaknesses? Do you seek help from God and others? Are you teachable? What ideas have you changed lately? Do you admit it when you make mistakes? Do you ask others as well as God to forgive you?

Sensitivity (Those Who Mourn): While the world says to kick up your heels and enjoy it all, Jesus says there is a time to grieve. But what kind of grieving?

(1) *We need to recognize and accept our own pains and sorrows in*

71

life. We then need to learn from them and grow from them, rather than pretend they don't exist. When we deny our pain, bitterness slowly builds up on the inside until the lid blows off. Some people laugh off any pain in a superficial unrealistic way. Thus, they never creatively handle their disappointments.

Only when we recognize and own our pains and sorrows can we give them over to God. And God wants us to do that: "Casting all your anxiety upon Him, because He cares for you" (1 Peter 5:7). Notice that the verse just before this one is, "Humble yourselves. . . ." Only the poor in spirit will let go of his anxieties. The proud keeps them because he thinks he can handle them alone. No wonder pride precedes a fall. Paul recognized his pains and sufferings and so depended upon the grace of God.

(2) *We need to recognize and share the sufferings and pains of others.* We dare not close our eyes to the hurts of others, but open our hearts and care. Jesus' life was filled with compassion, and so He invested His life in others. In that way, He did not permit His own sufferings to drown Him in His own sorrows. One of the finest ways to stay afloat is to reach out to others in need. Are you down in the dumps? Find someone who needs your help. You will discover quickly that helping them gives immediate help to yourself.

(3) *We need to be sensitive to the feelings of others.* It isn't enough to be sensitive to just the hurts and sufferings of other. We need also to be sensitive to the various feelings a person has or could have. Such sensitivity will reach out to protect the person from being crushed by thoughtless words or deeds. It will also help us to build up a person by using words that communicate the value of another. No one has a right to use his tongue, his actions, or his reactions to devastate a person's vulnerable feelings.

(4) *We need a sensitivity to our own feelings.* The person who understands his own feelings is less likely to allow those feelings to control his actions. Have you ever awakened in the morning feeling touchy for no reason at all? Knowing that can help prevent you from blaming someone else for angering you. Knowing what feelings you have that are very vulnerable can help you understand that you need patience when others carelessly trespass those vulnerable feelings

with recklessness. Sometimes we can be our own worst enemies. Being sensitive to feelings we have and other people
have can help us render control (to be meek, the next attitude
Jesus mentioned).

(5) *We need to grieve over our sins.* Then we will not write sins
off as trivial as we continue in them. Rather, we will begin to
move away from them, because we see how our sins hurt
God and others. And the hurt that our sins give to others
grieves us more than the fun sin gives to us.

(6) *We need to grieve over the sins of others.* Too few of us are
moved by the violence, greed, and abuse that goes on daily.
Thus, too few of us invest our lives to introduce people to the
Lord, who can convert people from habitual sins to become
growing saints. And too few of us take stands against im-
moral practices in our communities. Someone has observed
that all it takes for evil to succeed is for good men to do
nothing. Apathy about the sins of others paralyzes us to do
nothing.

The person who has inside sensitivity and compassion to
pains, suffering, and sin does not have to stand alone. God
promises to comfort. The word *comfort* literally means "call
alongside of." God hears our mourning and takes that as a
call to Him. And He stands alongside of us to hold us up. He
supports us. That's secure buoyancy.

Are you sensitive? Do you admit it when you are hurting?
Do you invest time, interest, and money to relieve the pain of
others? Do you let community leaders know your stand on
moral issues? Do you reach out to help victims of sin? Do you
understand people in sin and seek to be their friends and lead
them to greener pastures?

Calm (Meek): The word *meek* was used to describe a tame
stallion that was once wild. It described ointment that could
sooth stings. A meek person is under control and is able to
bring calm rather than strife. He is not aggressive. He does
not seek revenge. He is not self-assertive. He is not cold-
hearted. He does not take advantage of the vulnerable positions of others. He is willing to give up his rights if it would
benefit others. While the Jews pushed their status of race,
while the Romans pushed their position of power, and while
the Greeks pushed their advantage of knowledge, Jesus emptied himself and became a servant of others.

But won't the meek in this world lose out? Doesn't nature itself teach us that the earth belongs to the aggressors? No, not really! If that were true, then why do we no longer have the aggressive dinosaurs and saber-toothed tigers, while the meek sheep still graze on the hillsides? Doesn't the world belong to the grabbers, the demanders, and the manipulators? No, not really! This world belongs to God, as the psalmist declared, "The heavens are Thine, the earth is Thine: The world and all it contains . . ." (Psalm 89:11). This world is not to be grabbed from God, but to be given by God as a gift. And He has already bequeathed it to the meek. Calm people who are not out of control will be the heirs of the earth.

Are you meek? Do you forgive others and let them know? Do you resist defending yourself? Do you throw away negative letters? Do you refuse to meditate upon negative remarks said to you or about you? Do you overcome evil with good? Do you meditate upon God's promise that God (not you) will work all situations for the good and that God does not fail?

Right intentions (Hunger and Thirst for Righteousness): The buoyed up person keeps his intentions zeroed in on righteousness. Notice! Jesus didn't say that the buoyed up person is always right. Jesus never once said, "Blessed are those who always have to be right or always act right."

We are being taught by keen psychologists that our intentionalities are very strong factors that determine our present behavior. We become what we aim at. We aim at what we crave. Our crave can become our grave, but it doesn't have to.

To crave for righteousness is to crave for the personal presence of Jesus. He is the righteousness (1 Corinthians 1:30). Somehow we have reduced craving for righteousness to craving for right interpretations of the Bible, correctness in doctrine, and good morals. But we can emphasize correctness and still be very distant from a personal relationship, identity, comradeship, and oneness with the personal presence of Jesus.

Some cravings cannot be satisfied, like the live presence of a loved one who has died or the growth of a leg that has been amputated. But God promised a satisfaction when we crave for righteousness. He will fill us. But what will keep us from getting too full? Just one thing—sharing with others. We aren't to be a closed container of Jesus' presence, but a pipe-

74

line through whom right relationships enter and are channeled to others. We are like a pump that is full of water only to make that water available. The pump doesn't burst because of an unhealthy overfilling.

Are you craving for righteousness? Are you spending time with God's Word? Are you spending time in prayer—even when nothing is going wrong? Do you reach out to the neglected and seek to bring dignity to their lives? Are you an ambassador of God by introducing Him to people in a ministry of reconciliation? Are you involved in an active fellowship with God's people? Are you seeking to correct some social injustices and inequalities to people in your community?

Benevolence (Merciful): Mercy is the inner ache that always seeks an outer action to help a person in spiritual, emotional, social, or physical need. Mercy has sympathy for the suffering, and responds with services; pity for the pitiful, and responds with caring; hurting for the hurt, and responds with help. The person who is full of mercy to others is the buoyed up person because God promises to spend mercy on that person.

Are you merciful? Do you know of anyone hurting right now? Have you helped anyone in the immediate past?

Integrity (Pure in Heart): The pure in heart is not the person who is perfect. He is the person who is not doubled-minded or double-tongued. He doesn't say one thing but mean another. His outer action is not a facade that covers his real feelings. The pure in heart is transparent. What you see is what he is. He is not a phony.

He can see God in the world because his vision is not blurred by inner insincerity. He is not always reading hidden meanings in what he sees and hears. The impure in heart always projects his own double life onto others; so he cannot see God in their lives.

Are you pure in heart? Do you mean what you say? Do your compliments come from the inside? When you touch people outwardly, do you also touch them inwardly? Do you refuse to vacillate about saying good and bad things about someone, depending upon who is listening? Are your outer actions consistent with your inner attitudes?

Peaceableness (The Peacemaker): The breakers of peace are many. The makers of peace seem to be few. The makers of peace are active in reconciling individuals and groups who are out of harmony with each other. The makers of peace become bridges, not canyons. The makers of peace stop gossip by refusing to repeat it—even if it is true. They will not cut down others. They will take the initiative to patch up difficulties. They will not retaliate. They will not be critical of others. They will treat others as they wish to be treated. They will forgive. They will make decisions that benefit people who have hurt them. Are you a peacemaker?

Such a person is called a child of God because peacemaking pulls together many of the characteristics of God. And those who manifest God's characteristics are God's offspring, who have God's Spirit living inside and allow that Spirit to come out. They live by the sword of the Spirit, rather than by the spirit of the sword.

Endurance (The Persecuted). God's kind of attitudes are not always appreciated or applauded on earth, but they are in Heaven. While we are misunderstood on earth, we are understood in Heaven. While people may insult us here, Jesus honors us there. While we may get blasted here, we are being blessed there. So we are buoyed up, knowing that what happens negatively to us here because we stand for God will pass, but whatever happens to us positively in Heaven will last.

The buoyed up one sees the future beyond the present. He sees Heaven and rewards. And both of those are eternal.

Beautiful Activities

Inner attitudes are motivators for corresponding outer activities. The righteousness of Jesus' followers is to surpass the righteousness of the Pharisees. But how? Not by the external things we do or do not do, but by the inner motivations and attitudes that square with the outer actions. The Pharisees loved to keep the externals of the law while neglecting any change on the inside. For instance, they might not murder someone (external act), but they could remain angry (inner attitudes) at that person forever. They would not cut down a person with a knife, for that was against the law, but they would cut down a person in their thoughts and with their words. The kind of activities that surpasses the Pharisees will ooze out of Jesus' inner attitudes of buoyancy. Jesus mentions a few of those activities in the rest of this sermon. Let's take a brief look at them.

Refuse to belittle people (5:20-22).

We can belittle people with our thoughts—anger—and with our words—slander. But a person whose inner attitude squares with the beatitudes will not do that.

Make friends with opponents (5:23-26).

Don't feed on anger; don't use words to cut your opponents down, and don't wait on them to apologize. Do you want your opponents to initiate reconciliation? Then you are wanting the wrong thing. You are to be the one who makes friends.

Discipline your sexuality (5:27-30).

It isn't wrong to have desires when seeing an attractive person of the opposite sex. This text is speaking against feeding intentional desires of adultery. Literally, the Greek says, "Everyone who looks on a woman *for the purpose to lust . . . ."* It is the planned look with a perverted desire that is wrong. So don't make plans that would feed wrong desires and then follow up those plans.

Be committed to your mate (5:31, 32).

Do you know what hinders commitment to your married partner more than anything else—commitment to selfishness. Greek and Roman men lived primarily for themselves. How about today? How about you?

Make your word your bond (5:33-37).

Be so trustworthy that people instantly believe your promises without reservations.

Don't retaliate (5:38).

No one has to get even. Don't keep score.

Be extraordinarily vulnerable (5:39-42).

Be willing to absorb slander. A slap on the cheek was a degrading insulting act. Do more than what is expected; go the second mile. Be benevolent.

Seek the advancement of your enemies (5:43-48).

Agape love is the kind that seeks the well-being of another person. That's not so hard to do if that other person is a wife, child, friend, or someone else whom you know will return benefits back to you. But how about the antagonists? How well do you seek *their* well being?

Do what you do out of a commitment of service, not for status (6:1-4).

The greatest in God's kingdom are not necessarily those who give the most away, but those who give themselves away in service.

Pray for God's hearing, not man's (6:5-13).

Our prayers should lift up God, not ourselves. They should help people honor God's greatness, not our oratory. This model prayer includes several delightful aspects:

1. Relationship: "Our Father"
2. Recognition: "Who art"
3. Adoration: "hallowed"
4. Anticipation: "Thy kingdom come"
5. Consecration: "Thy will be done"
6. Universality: "on earth"
7. Conformity: "as it is"
8. Supplication: "give us"
9. Definiteness: "this day"
10. Necessity: "our daily bread"
11. Penitence: "forgive us"
12. Obligation: "debts"
13. Forgiveness: "as we"
14. Love and mercy: "debtor"
15. Guidance: "lead us"
16. Protection: "not into temptation"
17. Salvation: "deliver us"
18. Righteousness: "from evil"
19. Faith: "for Thine is the Kingdom"
20. Humility: "and the power"
21. Reverence: "and the glory"
22. Timelessness: "forever"
23. Affirmation: "Amen"—so be it

Forgive people (6:14, 15).

Do what you do with God's eyes in mind, not man's (6:16-18).

Isn't it easy to "bandstand" our Christianity so people will marvel at our involvement and sacrifice?

This doesn't mean that we should hide our Christianity under a bushel so no one will know. But it does mean that we do not do things *for the purpose* of being seen by men and honored by them. Honor from men may come. It's one thing to seek honor and grab it. It is another thing to receive it humbly as a gift. It is one thing to live for honor. But it is another thing to be honored for the way we have lived.

Be generous with financial resources (6:19-24).

We can be either grabbers or givers. We can be either stingy or generous, selfless or selfish. We can be either lovers of God or lovers of money.

Trust God for the necessities in life (6:25-34).

This doesn't mean that we become lazy and say, "Okay, God, let's have all those essentials." Paul wrote that a person who will not work should not be fed (2 Thessalonians 3:10). Jesus is not saying, "Don't work," but He is saying, "Get your priorities straight. Seek first the kingdom of God and His righteousness. Don't worry."

God gives us that insight for our own health. Dr. Edward Podolsky has substantiated the correlation between worry and heart trouble, some forms of asthma, ulcers, colds, high blood pressure, thyroid problems, migraine headaches, arthritis, and numerous stomach disorders (Dr. Edward Podolsky, *Stop Worrying and Get Well*, New York: Bernard Ackerman, Inc. 1944).

When God tells us to quit worrying, He isn't telling us not to be concerned. But He is saying that we should not be immoderately concerned. The word *worry* comes from a Greek word that literally means to divide the mind. We can tell when concern turns into worry when our minds are divided between trust, which gives us assurance, and doubt, which gives us neurotic uncertainty. Then our minds become distracted and our energies get diverted to negative and destructive thoughts.

Worry displays immaturity of faith. For worry suggests the following: that we do not accept the fact that God can and does meet our needs (Matthew 6:25-32), that He doesn't do all things well (Mark 7:37), that He doesn't work all things for good (Romans 8:28), that He doesn't supply all our needs (Philippians 4:19), and that He doesn't care for us (1 Peter 5:7). Worry is a confession that our faith believes that our God is too small.

Don't condemn others (7:1-5).

Isn't it easy for us to see the bad in others while seeing only the good in ourselves? And isn't it difficult to see the good in others and the bad in ourselves?

Don't be reckless with what is holy (7:6).

There are times to share the pearl of great price (the gospel), and there are times not to. We need to be discriminating. Jesus remained silent before Pilate's cynical worldliness. He knew His audience was not ready.

Be proactive (7:7-11).

Don't just sit around wishing—ask, seek, and knock.

Treat people the way you want them to treat you (7:12).

Make selective decisions (7:13, 14).

Don't just go with the flow. What's popular may lead to destruction.

Be selective about whom you follow (7:15-23).

Too many today follow the success image, the Madison Avenue profile, the good speakers, the entertainers, or those with a team of writers, P. R. men, and the like. God expects us to do a bit of investigation before we throw our moral and financial support onto somebody's bandwagon—even though it seems that everybody else is doing so. Remember the masses are not always right.

Be a doer and not just a hearer (7:24-27).

We can become professional sponges, soaking up but never giving out. God is interested in our hearing only because hearing is necessary for doing. Be a doer of the Word, not just a listener of words.

Do sermons really change you? Do lessons make a difference? Does Bible reading alter your thinking, feelings, and behavior? Why listen and read?

The attitudes Jesus spoke about are His own. He freely offers them to us through His own Holy Spirit, who lives inside us Christians. To have Jesus' Spirit is to have His nature in seed form. But we must be willing to let that seed grow so that in all aspects we grow up into Christlikeness.

As newborn people, we have been recreated in the image of Christ (2 Corinthians 5:17; Ephesians 4:24; Colossians 3:10). But unless we expose ourselves to the environment of Christ, some of His attitudinal and behavioral characteristics may not develop. Let us not allow the non-Christlikeness of the environment to mold us into its image.

Let's be Christ's children—imitators of Him—as we follow Him—inside out.

Application

The apostles soon penetrated the world of their day as disciples of Jesus. As they did, they encountered actions and reactions that hurt. They heard words that could have put them into the pits. They faced the kind of rejection that could have caused them to feel like total failures in self worth. How did they stay afloat through it all?

Jesus had outlined the way for them. And that way was not only for them; it is also for us.

Life will throw all of us its curves. Haven't you ever had hurts, disappointments, setbacks, disillusionments, and rejections in your family, with friends, at your work, in the community, and in the church?

We can let those experiences bitter us or better us. We can shrivel up in those times or we can grow up. If we dwell upon the negative aspects of the person who has hurt us, or if we dwell upon the details of the hurt, we will go into a tailspin that hurls us toward an emotional crash. The longer we do that, the closer we move from depression to manic depression; from anger to violence; from withdrawal to rejection.

What steps can we take to prevent any disappointing circumstances around us (family, friends, career, community, or church) from doing that to us?

The first step is to commit our minds to meditate upon the right things. Often our depression, anger, or rebellion is heightened during the lonely hour when we have time to think. We must control those times and not let them control us. The psalmist spoke often about the importance of proper meditation.

When I remember Thee on my bed,
I meditate on Thee in the night watches.
For Thou hast been my help
And in the shadow of Thy wings I sing for joy.
My soul clings to Thee;
Thy right hand upholds me.

Psalm 63:6-8

Thy Word I have treasured in my heart,
That I may not sin against Thee.

Psalm 119:11

Even though princes sit and talk against me,
Thy servant meditates on Thy statutes.
Thy testimonies also are my delight;
They are my counselors.

Psalm 119:23, 24

May the arrogant be ashamed, for they subvert me with a lie;
But I shall meditate on Thy precepts.

Psalm 119:78

But upon what can we meditate that would be helpful in times of disappointment when we would like to retaliate. How about meditating upon the beautiful attitudes of the beatitudes and begin a mental plan for application of them to our present circumstances. Meditate upon the following:

1. *Poor in Spirit*—Think, "God I need your guidance: I admit I am a small child who thinks I have all the answers, but I don't. I do not want to act or react according to the desires of the flesh. Slow me down to submit to Your way as a humble, trusting, obedient child."

2. *Mourning*—Think, "Father, here is where I am hurting. Because I recognize that, I can cast this hurt upon You. You have asked me to cast all my anxiety upon You, because You really care about me (1 Peter 5:7). You promised that Jesus would hear my griefs and carry my sorrows. So I give these that I recognize to You so You can help me take my eyes off of self-hurt and invest energy and interest in others."

Then begin to think about the needs of the person or situation that has hurt you. Meditate upon the needs that person has. And then commit yourself to begin meeting those needs that you can. It may be something like the need for recognition, for appreciation, for kind words, for forgiveness, for patience, or for freedom. If it's a need you can meet, meet it.

3. *Gentle*—Meditate upon being calm in reactions and soothing to people. Think of specific ways to express gentleness. Picture yourself doing that. Commit yourself in meditation to transfer the picture into real life.

4. *Craving for righteousness*—Refuse to think about self justification or self defense. Think about initiating and maintaining right relationships with God and with people. Make that your burning want. Some persons may not respond

82

positively; nevertheless, be the kind of person that initiates the right relationships.

5. *Merciful*—Think about being filled with mercy and about ways to express that. That may include forgiveness or doing the unexpected without demanding or expecting appreciation for it.

6. *Pure in heart*—Meditate upon drawing together your actions and attitudes into a single package. If those attitudes don't square with Jesus', then don't act hastily. Wait! Keep meditating and feeding upon God's Word—particularly upon the Sermon on the Mount—and wait to act until you can decide on a kind of behavior that would reflect the attitudes of the beatitudes.

Often, we think we have to have the attitude completely nailed down first, *then* the behavior follows. But that's not always true. As attitudes feed behavior, so does behavior feed attitudes. If you don't have that attitude, but know that a certain kind of behavior would reflect that attitude—then behave in that manner *with the commitment that you want that attitude to be formed in you.* Feelings and attitudes often follow behavior if *we want them to.*

7. *Peacemaking*—Meditate upon what you need to think and feel, and how you need to behave in order to make and maintain an environment of harmony. This doesn't guarantee that every other person will follow suit. In fact, some kind of persecution (emotional or physical) could follow. But decide that from your side, you will bring peace to your own heart first and then to the situation, as much as that situation will permit.

If you will apply the beatitudes to any situation, changes will result. The situation may not become what you desire, but you will change.

That's what Paul was getting at when he told us to exult in tribulations, for they bring perseverance, and perseverance brings proven character, and proven character brings hope, and hope does not disappoint us because God's love lives in our hearts (Romans 5:3-5).

It's not easy to exult in tribulations (pressures), but in them—if we meditate upon, and apply, God's attitudes—our characters mature, pessimism turns into optimism (hope), and room we have in our heart for grudges, retaliation, and hate is filled instead with God's kind of love. And although the outer circumstances may not change, it is a better, brighter world we wake up to and live through. His attitudes planted, cultivated, and applied make all the difference in the world.

And when the storm is past, you will still be floating, while others may have sunk to the bottom long before.

Indeed, Jesus gave His disciples a recipe for living through the ups and downs of life. In short, that recipe is to take one's eyes and thoughts off self.

My secretary has a beautiful picture in front of her desk that I can see when my door is open, as it usually is. It is a picture of Jesus walking on the water, although the storm is fierce all around Him.

I often look at that picture and think Jesus wants me also to walk on the water. God is not in the sinking business. He is an expert in floating and walking on the water. And He has outlined how I too can float and walk rather than sink and drown.

Apply the beatitudes in meditation and then in practice, and you will discover that God knows what He is doing.

Next to that picture of Jesus walking on the water is a plaque with words that summarize what we have said in this chapter.

> Where there is faith
> there is love
> Where there is love
> there is peace
> Where there is peace
> there is God
> Where there is God
> there is no need.
> (Anonymous)

Too many times, we want the *other* person to have faith in God and us, and to express love to us. Then we think there will be peace. But the secret is not in manipulating and controlling the *other* person, but in self. *We* must have the faith and *we* must express love. Then peace will emerge—inner peace. And we will practice the presence of God.

The Beautiful Masses

(Matthew 8–9)

When God created the Grand Canyon with all of its awesomeness, He declared, "It is good." When He put together the Pacific and Atlantic Oceans with the beauty of the full moon reflecting off the water and the waves kissing the beaches, He said, "It is good." When He created the Alps, the Sierras, and the Rockies with their impressionable pictures of majestic strength married to the soothing sight of the snow caps, God pronounced, "It is good." When He structured the sky with a backdrop of blue, dotted at times with clouds, brightened by day with the sun and sparkling by night with the moon and diamond-like stars, the Creator announced, "It is good."

But only when God put people—in the plural—on planet earth did He ever say, "It is *very* good." Only people are eternal. People are the summit of God's creation and the target of God's love. Wherever you find people, you will find the love of God. Wherever you find more people, you will find more of the love of God.

Jesus and the Multitudes

When Jesus saw the multitudes, He went to the mountain and began to teach His disciples the attitudes and activities they would need to keep them afloat (Matthew 5–7). However, ministry to the multitudes cannot be fulfilled by just saying sermons on a mountain.

So Jesus came down from the mountain (8:1). To say it in a modern way, He came down from the mountain to the valley where there were long lines, pushing, yelling, cheating, unemployment, sickness, cars honking, five-miles-per-hour freeway traffic, and smog. And there He saw the multitudes again. But what did He see? Did He see just crowds that got in His way, masses of hurried people who were arrogant, selfish faces without names and needs?

Oh, no! When Jesus saw the multitudes, He looked beyond the numbers and saw people—real people with names and feelings and needs. He saw people's kids, parents, grandparents, husbands, and wives. He saw people who had special joys and burdened sorrows. He saw people who were active, but without meaningful purpose. He saw people who were hurrying, but they were really wandering around like sheep without a shepherd. He saw people who needed to be loved by someone who really cared. And He saw people that a loving, caring person could lead to a life more abundant.

We can't miss it. When Jesus saw the multitudes, He saw people who were hurting and needed help. A leper came to Him wanting help (Matthew 8:2). A centurion needed help (Matthew 8:5-13). When Jesus got away for a bit of a retreat, He saw that Peter's mother-in-law needed help (Matthew 8:14-17). His own disciples needed help (Matthew 8:23-27). He saw two men with demons who needed help (Matthew 8:28-34). A paralytic needed help (Matthew 9:1-7). A synagogue official needed help (Matthew 9:18-26). Two blind men and a dumb man needed help (Matthew 9:27-33).

Do you get the picture? Jesus saw more than just crowds, something to complain about. He saw opportunities to express the love of God. What happened when He saw the multitudes is summed up in Matthew 9:36, "And seeing the multitudes, He felt compassion for them." That means their hurts became His; their passion became His; their needs became His.

Us and the Multitudes

How do we see the multitudes? Is it possible that we too easily see them as the blind man whom Jesus touched saw people in Mark 8:22-26? Jesus touched that blind man, and then asked Him a question, "Do you see anything?" and that man looked up and said, "I see men, for I am seeing them like trees, walking about."

Do we see people more like trees than people? To see people like trees is to see life but without feelings to consider. I've never tried to guard my actions to protect the feelings of any tree. How about of people? To see people like trees is to see life without souls to save. I've never tried to lead a tree to faith, repentance, and baptism. How about non-Christian people? How many have you talked with about Jesus lately? To see people like trees is to see life but with no need for forgiveness. I have never offered forgiveness to any tree. And some have done me in. Are you holding any grudges against people? To see people like trees is to see life without the need of friends. I spend little time trying to befriend trees, understand them, talk with them, or be their companions. How many friends are you making with people? To see people like trees is to see them like things to manipulate, use, abuse, neglect, and reject when their usefulness to us is over. To see people like trees is to see them more the way a computer is programmed by man to see them rather than the way Christ empowered by God's Spirit sees them.

Unless we see people correctly and respond to them with the love of God, we sink in the waves of the crowd. We float by applying the beautiful attitudes and activities of the Sermon on the Mount.

Notice that Jesus saw individuals in the crowds in an unprejudiced way. No one was too insignificant for Him to notice. A leper was a social outcast, and Jesus cared about him. A centurion had social status, and Jesus cared about him, too. Not only is it easy to neglect the down and out, it is also easy to ignore the up and out. It is so comfortable to reach out only to those like us. But Jesus knew that all people, regardless of their social standings, shared many common needs and had many universal feelings.

From the traditional standpoint in Jesus' day, the leper had the wrong kind of disease, the centurion had the wrong kind of career (Jews belittled Roman soldiers), the centurion was the wrong race (a Gentile), and Peter's mother-in-law was the wrong sex (Jews and Greeks disparaged and sometimes maligned women). But those "wrong kinds" made no difference to Jesus because He was the "right kind" of person, filled with the beautiful attitudes of the beatitudes.

He was poor in spirit; so He related to those far below Him in status. He mourned; so He was sensitive to needs around Him. He was meek; so He didn't go out of control when He was sharply criticized (Matthew 9:11-13). He craved for righteousness; so He reached out in relationships. He was merciful; so He acted to relieve the hurts of others. He was pure in heart; so He had no hidden self-serving motives. He was willing to be persecuted; so He went against the social traditions and prejudices and stood outside some social guidelines for meeting peoples' needs. For instance, He healed on the Sabbath.

Needs, the Multitudes, and Faith

As Jesus expressed no prejudice in the kinds of people He loved, so He had no bias in the kinds of needs He met. No need was too impossible for His personal care. In the first century, no doctor had a cure for paralysis. But that did not discourage Jesus.

That centurion really had to have a mammoth faith to come to Jesus with an uncrossable mountain for Jesus to remove. He probably rehearsed his one-to-one "prayer" many times before reaching Jesus. But notice what happens. He didn't even get a chance to finish his prayer. He starts it by saying, "Lord, my servant is lying paralyzed at home, suffering pain" (Matthew 8:6). Then Jesus interrupts him. "I will come and heal him." That guy didn't even get a chance to ask.

But notice something else. Just because Jesus knew what that official wanted, He waited to promise healing until after the centurion acknowledged his own humility and confessed faith that God was big enough to do anything. That is seen in that centurion's first word, "Lord." Today, we think we are big enough to handle anything. So why bring God in? We also think certain problems are too big for God. Oh, we would not admit that openly, but our prayer lives and testimonial lives demonstrate it. Are we willing to humiliate ourselves enough to ask God for some impossibles, and even let others know that's our faith-stand? Jesus told that leader, "Let it be done to you as you have believed." He later said to two blind men, "Be it done to you according to your faith" (Matthew 9:29). If everything God did in our lives and for us corresponded exactly with our faith, we would really be bad off. I thank God that His love usually goes beyond our faith. When we see His hand working out things in those situations, it stretches our faith. However, we probably keep God from doing unbelievable things in us and for us because of our littleness of faith. Are *you* setting faith-goals and asking God for them in trust? Remember, faith is described as the assurance of *things* hoped for, the conviction of *things* not seen (Hebrews 11:1). What specific objective things do you have conviction about receiving? Do you have a living hope for specifics because of your faith? Too often, our faith is in generalities. We have faith, but not for anything specific. A church that does not have faith goals for specifics will probably receive little of God's extraordinary acts that await our faith for activation. And so it is with an individual Christian. Our lack of an expanding faith for God's intervention and involvement in our lives keeps Him at arm's length. While we have salvation, we miss the grandeur of His power and might.

Notice something else about that centurion. His faith in Jesus' ability was so enormous that he did not have to have some kind of sensational act performed. "Just say the word, and my servant will be healed." If we had more faith like that, we would have fewer religious con artists around. Do you know one reason why the sensationalist, religious charlatons multiply and line their monetary pockets? Because God's people do not have enough faith to say to God in prayer, "Just say the word. That's enough. If You choose not to, I accept that. For You do all things well." The day I am writing this chapter, our newspaper reported that one of T.V.'s most popular charismatic miracle workers spent a few days in Florida in a hotel suite that cost $1,000 a day. What's so tragic about that is this man's particular program raises millions of dollars a year from many people on social security and welfare, and from many who cannot afford a $100 a month utility bill.

Perhaps we need some "pastors of prayer" in our churches. These would be pastors who would help us grow in faith in God and in prayer faith. How much does not happen because we do not pray? I wonder how shocked (and perhaps shamed) we might be if Jesus should reveal it to us when He returns. I wonder what the heavenly program "This Is Your Life" would show if the films of our lives would be rewound and stopped at certain situations? Then Jesus would say "Here's what *would have* happened had you prayed. You simply did not ask—and keep asking in faith."

As no need was too *impossible* for Jesus, so no need was too *insignificant* for His time, interest, and personal involvement. Jesus not only performed awe-inspiring healings—like for the paralytic—but He also met simple, ho-hum needs. One day some children were brought to Jesus "so that He might lay His hands on them and pray" (Matthew 19:13-15). Jesus' disciples thought the children's needs were too insignificant for Jesus' attention, and they protested this waste of Jesus' time. But Jesus didn't see the children as a waste of time. Their needs were not too unimportant for His attention. Mark (10:14) tells us Jesus was "indignant" with His disciples for thinking that way. "And He took them in His arms and began blessing them, laying His hands on them" (Mark 10:16).

Jesus never met an unimportant person nor encountered an insignificant need. How easy it is for us to get so important that we become untouchable for people with needs. It is even possible for some pastors to become harder to contact than busy doctors, lawyers, or politicians. It is possible to get too busy to care.

Jesus saw the multitudes, but He did more than see. He interacted with the multitudes. He spoke to the multitudes. He served the multitudes. When He saw multitudes, He wasn't filled with contempt, apathy, indifference, and detachment. He was filled with compassion. And He expressed that compassion in practical ways. Notice the correlation. Jesus was filled with compassion (Matthew 9:36); the multitudes were filled with awe (Matthew 9:8), and marvelled (Matthew 9:33). No wonder the multitudes gathered to Him (Matthew 13:2) and followed Him (Matthew 12:15).

Jesus' Commission

After this initial encounter with the multitudes, Jesus sent His disciples to the multitudes to care about them as He did with the compassion of God (Matthew 10). That continues to be Jesus' charge to His disciples. He calls us to see and to care. He calls us to see spiritual needs of people separated from God and to bring them into a oneness with God (Matthew 28:19, 20; 2 Corinthians 5:17-20). He calls us to see the hurts of people around us—and to care (Matthew 25:35-46). In Matthew 25 Jesus talks about caring for people with a social stigma (in prison), a friendship problem (strangers), health problems (sick), and financial problems (hungry and thirsty). No person is too important or too insignificant, and no need is too impossible or too common for our sensitivity and our servanthood commitment.

How are you seeing the multitudes—as people created in the image of God or things like trees? Let us so care that people can say to us these words:

> I love you not only for what you are, but for what I am when I am with you.
> I love you for accepting me for who I am. I love you for looking deeply into my life and seeing all the good that no one else looks long enough to find.
> I love you for not highlighting all those weak things that you cannot help but notice.
> I love you for not being a perfectionist and for not nitpicking at all the ways I do not live up to your expectations.
> I love you because you are you and because He—Jesus—first loved us.
> I love you because you allow that compassion and love of Jesus to flow through you to me.
> I love you because you see me as a ME and not as a *tree.*

Something happened when I was a control tower supervisor in Japan that I can never forget. Two jet fighters were flying in formation and had just started their descent when the leader pilot radioed, "I've just lost my wing man." Immediately, we picked up the red crash phone that was connected to the rescue helicopter team on stand-by duty. When that phone is lifted, a rescue helicopter is to be in the air within 120 seconds.

The lead pilot descended below the clouds to look for his wing man, and when he found him, the wing man had bailed out and was in the ocean. The radio communications from that pilot stabbed our hearts as we listened.

"My wing man is in the water, but he is tangled up in his parachute line. *Have you notified* the helicopter?"

"He's floating, but having a difficult time getting his life raft inflated. *Have you commissioned* the helicopter?"

Minutes later:

"He's still not got an inflation. He's beginning to go under the water. *Where's the rescue team?*"

Minutes later:

"Now he's above the water, but still struggling. *Where's the helicopter?*"

Minutes later:

"He is now under the water again. *Where's the helicopter?*"

Seconds later:

"He's now about four to five feet under. I don't know if he can come up again. *Where is the helicopter?*"

Seconds later:

"I can't see him now! We've lost him! *Where is the helicopter?*"

Where was the helicopter? It never got to the scene. At the investigation and hearing it was discovered that the rescue team had decided to take the helicopter to a major military PX fifty miles away and do some Christmas shopping. That team was so busy taking care of selves that it got beyond the range of hearing the cries for help.

The multitudes are all around us. Many are already in the water without an inflated life raft, and the parachute lines of complex living are entangling them. Some are still floating. Others are beginning to sink.

Where are the rescue teams? Let us respond, "We are coming! We are here with the love and compassion of God!"

Check Your COMMITMENT
Studies from Matthew

9

by Knofel Staton

Walking on the Water

(Matthew 14:22-33)

"Everyday with Jesus is sweeter than the day before." Ever sing that song? Do you believe it? I don't. It is sheer fantasy and not fact.

Some T.V./radio preachers may make such a promise to the audience, but the Bible doesn't. In fact, the Bible records that some really bitter days can come right on the heels of sweet days for God's grand champions.

As the Christian has no right to look at the sweet days and conclude, "Boy, that proves I'm really pleasing God today," so does he have no right to interpret the bitter days with the observation, "I must have done something wrong. God is punishing me. I've got to confess sin and guilt to get my life right with God again."

Surely we can understand this by observing what happened to Jesus day after day. Some of His days were really sour. He was misunderstood, criticized, ignored, rejected, and blasphemed. The day with Pilate was not sweeter than the day before. The day on the cross was more bitter, not sweeter, than the day before. Paul talked about days he had during which nothing seemed to go right.

> "To this present hour we are both hungry and thirsty, and are poorly clothed, and are roughly treated, and are homeless; and we toil, working with our own hands; when we are reviled, we bless; when we are persecuted, we endure" (1 Corinthians 4:11-13).
> "We are afflicted in every way, but not crushed; perplexed, but not despairing; persecuted, but not forsaken; struck down, but not destroyed" (2 Corinthians 4:8, 9).
> "Are they servants of Christ? (I speak as if insane) I more so; in far more labors, in far more imprisonments, beaten times without

number, often in danger of death. Five times I received from the Jews thirty-nine lashes. Three times I was beaten with rods, once I was stoned, three times I was shipwrecked, a night and a day I spent in the deep. I have been on frequent journeys, in dangers from rivers, dangers from robbers, dangers from my countrymen, dangers from the Gentiles, dangers in the city, dangers in the wilderness, dangers on the sea, dangers among false brethren; I have been in labor and hardship, through many sleepless nights, in hunger and thirst, often without food, in cold and exposure. Apart from such external things, there is the daily pressure upon me of concern for all the churches" (2 Corinthians 11:23-38).

Now don't tell me Paul was describing one big fantastic marvelous honeymoon that he was experiencing in God's service.

God has not promised us that the skies will always be blue, but He has promised us, in the words of Annie Flint, "strength for the day, rest for the labor, and light for the way."

Athletes know the value of hanging in there even when they are hurting. Lou Gehrig played in over 2,030 consecutive baseball games. Was that because he was a superman who never felt sick or hurt? No! After he retired, his hands were x-rayed, and it was discovered that every finger of both hands had been broken at least once. But he didn't call in sick. He didn't throw in the towel. No one ever knew that he played with broken fingers.

Have you ever heard a boxer coming out of the ring saying, "I can't believe it. Do you know what he did? He actually hit me in that ring?" Have you ever heard a football player coming off the field shaking his head saying, "What's this world coming to? Everytime I get the ball, I get hit and it hurts." Do you know why football players get tackled? Because they carry the ball. Christians who carry the ball for God will get tackled, and if we come off the Christian ball field shaking our heads in disbelief because some sensational preacher said the Christian life is always a bed of roses, then we had better turn him off and turn God on. Peter wrote, "Beloved, do not be surprised at the fiery ordeal among you ... as though some strange thing were happening to you" (1 Peter 4:12).

Paul did not write about sweetness but about bitterness when he asked, "Who shall separate us from the love of Christ? Shall tribulation, or distress, or persecution, or famine, or nakedness, or peril, or sword" (Romans 8:35)? What's Paul talking about there? He's talking about the reality of singing something like, "Some days with Jesus are the pits—more bitter than the days before. But God loves me, and I'm not quitting God."

Paul was not talking about good days when he wrote, "For even when we came to Macedonia our flesh had no rest, but we were afflicted on every side: conflicts without, fears within" (2 Corinthians 7:5). He was not describing a "glory-halleluia day" when he wrote, "We were burdened excessively, beyond our strength, so that we despaired even of life" (2 Corinthians 1:8). Paul knew that carrying the ball for Jesus meant to be hurt—sometimes physically and sometimes emotionally.

Wayne Smith of Lexington, Kentucky, has said, "If you don't bleed, you are not blessed. If it doesn't cost, it doesn't count. God had only one Son without sin, but no son without sorrow."

One of our problems today is that Christians want to walk out on the church, give up any services for people, and crawl into a shell of isolation when their feelings get hurt and when people misunderstand, misjudge, and mistreat them. Jesus was terribly misunderstood, misjudged, and mistreated on the cross. He was not appreciated, but He didn't quit. He said, "Follow me!" But there is not much of a traffic jam around the cross these days. We like the "Disneylands" of Christianity where everything is positive, fun, thrilling, and sensational.

God's people will get knocked down, but we can refuse to be knocked out. We can walk on the water. We don't have to sink. Our God is a water-walking God, and He lives in us. In Him we, too, can walk on the water though the waves rage around us. Peter learned that lesson one unforgettable day with Jesus.

It had been one of those super-tough days—the kind that makes you want just to do nothing, think nothing, and go nowhere. Ever have days like that? Jesus and His disciples had experienced deep grief and loss. The word had reached them that John the Baptizer had been beheaded. Yet, they put in long hours that day teaching crowds over fifteen thousand (five thousand men plus women and children), and then feeding that many people. What a day it had been. The disciples just wanted to get away from people for a while. Ever have times like that?

After such a hard day of work coupled with grief, surely God would honor them with some protected peace and rest. But instead of sweet serenity came a severe storm. And it came in the line of duty. The disciples were obeying the command of Jesus to go ahead of Him to the other side of the lake. In spite of the fact that their location, environment, and activities were all a direct result of their obeying Jesus, the storm came.

Storms in life will come when we are doing everything right as well as when we are not. Why should we be surprised at that? Jesus said that God "causes His sun to rise on the evil and the good, and sends rain on the righteous and the unrighteous? (Matthew 5:45).

That lake wasn't large—about five miles across. But that's not the issue. A person can drown in a bathtub. The lake was small, but their boat was much smaller. They were in a crisis and needed help. And sure enough, Jesus came. But He came in a way beyond their finest hopes. He came walking on the water. The winds were tossing the boat, but not Jesus. Those waves lapped around His ankles like a puppy dog that playfully licks the heels of its master.

What an unexpected way to see Jesus. But Jesus is always coming to us in the storms of our lives. Sometimes we put our attention so much on the details of the storms—high bills, sickness, rejection, trouble with the kids, loss of a job, death, or a terminal disease—that we don't see Him coming to us. The disciples nearly missed Him on that day.

But still He came. And He comes today just as He came then—still walking on the water. And He comes saying, "Take courage, it is I; do not be afraid" (Matthew 14:27). God has come to meet you in the midst of the storm.

Peter saw that Jesus wasn't sinking and wanted to come to Jesus on the water. Isn't that the heartbeat of us all? None of us in the storm wants to run away from Jesus. Jesus' invitation was simple: "Come!"

Peter never doubted. He didn't say, "I can't do that. No one in my family has ever done that. Everybody I know crashes in when the crises come. My peers don't display such bold faith.

They don't risk. I'm going to play it safe as the other eleven. I'll make no promise. I'll make no commitment that could embarrass me. I'll just stay in the boat."

Instead of rationalizations, instead of cutting God down to Peter's size, instead of letting dimensions of science rule, Peter just did it. And again God honored, "As you believe, be it unto you."

As Peter put his feet to the water, he made an extraordinary faith decision. It wasn't just a repeat of what he had done before. This day was going to be different with Peter. He began to walk on the water in spite of the waves, winds, limitations of science, past traditions, loneliness of the decision (no one else was doing it), and the irrationality of it. He stepped out on faith to do something that he knew was bigger than he. To do that was Peter's vote that he really liked God. Is it possible that a lot of Christians do not really like God as much as we claim. We like to be in control. We are uncomfortable with anyone or anything that we can't control. No man can control God. We can't get Him chained to our constitution, by-laws, creeds, traditions, or limitations. So our faith is too often a vote of confidence in our limitations. And we are ready to crucify anyone else who dares to do the impossible. Could that be one reason the religious leaders masterminded the crucifixion of Jesus? Jesus did the impossible, and in so doing He threatened the limitations the religious leaders had and the boxes they had put God inside. After all, Jesus' extraordinary faith and the extraordinary deeds He did because of his faith would surely cause extraordinary growth. The religious leaders would have to open themselves to a bigger God, or criticize Jesus and claim that His extraordinary deeds were really the workings of the devil (interesting that the devil has power, but not God), or, eventually, kill Him. And they tried it all, because they enjoyed controlling the littleness of their limitations more than the risk of a God they could not contain.

When Jesus walked on water, He did what man cannot do. When He invited Peter to come, He invited Peter to do what man cannot do.

Why should it surprise us to believe, teach, and practice that God can do the impossible? Isn't that our first exposure to God? He created the world out of nothing. Then what would be impossible for Him to do in the world? Throughout the Bible, God's limitlessness is affirmed.

Is anything too difficult for the Lord? (Genesis 18:14).
Nothing is too difficult for Thee (Jeremiah 32:17).
Behold I am the Lord, the God of all flesh; is anything too difficult for Me? (Jeremiah 32:27).

God created out of nothing. He caused a flood that covered the whole planet. He parted the Red Sea. He saw to it that His people walked the wilderness for forty years with the same sandals and clothing that did not wear out. He caused women to get pregnant years after they stopped menstruation and years after their husbands became impotent. He caused a virgin to become pregnant without male sperm. He healed the incurable, raised the dead, calmed the storms, and walked on water.

The Christian age began with a special messenger from Heaven declaring, "For nothing will be impossible with God" (Luke 1:37). And that wasn't past tense, but future tense. God is still all powerful. An ugly canyon of Christianity is continually being dug by the littleness of our faith, which chips away at the bigness of God's ability.

Peter began to walk on the water. But then he took his eyes off the all-powerful Jesus. He began to feel the wind, see the waves, and observe the boat still tossing threateningly. Then he probably turned his thoughts to the limitations of self and past experiences. "I can't really be doing this. I've bitten off more than I can chew." And so Peter began to sink. But he still didn't give up on Jesus. He cried out, "Lord, save me!"

And immediately Jesus stretched out his hand and took hold of Peter. Jesus seized Peter but also scolded him. "O you of little faith, why did you doubt?" (It is clear that Peter's sinking was caused by Peter's doubt.) We believe to float. We doubt to sink.

There is something that is easy to miss in this event. When Peter stepped out of that boat, he was at least willing to take the risk. He was willing to take whatever risks were involved in answering Jesus' one word challenge, "Come!" Are we willing to take any risks for God? Some of us need to get out of our boats and get our feet wet. God is not willing for us to sink.

Have you ever wondered how Peter got back to the boat? Matthew doesn't say he walked back on top of the water. Perhaps Jesus carried him. Isn't that a beautiful scene? The big, muscular, rugged fisherman in the arms of Jesus, who continued to walk on the water. What humility and submission and trust that took from Peter. Although Peter's faith was too little for him to continue to walk on the water, it was still big enough to believe that Jesus could continue walking on water. And in Jesus' arms, Peter would not sink.

The question is, are we willing to get out of our safety boats and walk on water because we believe in God, more than ourselves? Are we willing to submit ourselves and the weight of our cares and plans, pasts and futures to that One who comes to us walking on water? Or do we burden our little ships down with the excess baggage of worry, doubt, and pessimism? Do we compare the smallness of our boat with the severity of the storm and then expect to sink any second?

The God who created this universe is a God of buoyancy.

Got any rivers you think are uncrossable?
God any mountains you can't tunnel through?
God specializes in things thought impossible;
He does the things others cannot do.

("Got Any Rivers," © Copyright 1945. Renewal 1972 by Oscar Eliason. Assigned to Singspiration, a division of the Zondervan Corporation. All rights reserved. Used by permission.

Lightening the Load

(Matthew 12:1-14; 15:1-9)

Let's pretend for just a moment that you are standing along the railing of the sinking Titanic. The last life raft has pulled away from the ship. And you know that if you are going to survive, you will have to jump overboard and stay above the water until you are rescued.

For several minutes before you jump into the water, people around you are giving you their keepsakes to take with you. One ties an antique clock around your waist. Another ties a jewelry box to your left leg. Another ties a packet of books to your right leg. Another ties a waterproof picture album to your neck. Another slips a knapsack over your shoulder filled with things that he has collected over the years. A little child hands you his favorite teddy bear.

How much of that will you take with you? Will you make it a priority to keep intact everything people handed over to you because you do not want to offend anyone? So into the water you jump with all the hand-me-downs.

Let's pretend a bit further. Let's suppose that by your strength, you kept afloat with all that excess baggage. Then, within a few minutes, you are picked up by a large lifeboat that can hold one hundred people. However, only twenty people are in it. You make twenty-one. However, you are the last person that boat can take because it not only has twenty-one people in it, but also multitudes of bulky keepsakes that people on the Titanic handed down to those getting into the life rafts.

As the lifeboat progresses through the water, it passes hundreds of people in the water who must get into a lifeboat for survival, but there is no room on the lifeboat because it is weighted and overcrowded with hand-me-downs. The people who treasure those hand-me-downs are now gone; nevertheless, the people in the lifeboat feel they have a commitment to keep those hand-me-downs at all costs. The twenty-one survivors have voted to keep the hand-me-downs even though keeping them in the boat will keep people crowded out.

An exaggeration? A wild imagination? If you think so, then sit with me in the church. And as you sit in the church, begin to observe all the hand-me-downs (traditions) that have become our priority to keep and protect. In fact, survivors in the Christian life raft will fight each other to keep the keepsakes. Some have even thrown fellow survivors overboard who questioned keeping the hand-me-downs. Protecting the hand-me-downs has become more important for many than picking up the drowning survivors around us.

Jesus faced that kind of mentality in His day. The first time fellow travelers in His boat secretly planned to throw Him overboard was when He wanted to discard one of the weighty hand-me-downs to make room for another person. "But the Pharisees went out, and counseled together against Him, as to how they might destroy Him" (Matthew 12:14). Why? Because Jesus set aside a hand-me-down to heal a man with a withered hand (Matthew 12:9-14). It is one thing to use the Sabbath as a tool for worship, but it is another thing to worship the Sabbath. We are masters over whatever we use as a tool. But we become mastered by whatever we worship. Too many tools that can be discarded in the church have become idols to protect and preserve at all cost.

Jesus called these "traditions" (Matthew 15:2). The word *tradition* literally means something handed down. There is nothing wrong with traditions. We are all the result of, and work with, what others have handed down to us. But there is something terribly wrong when traditions control our worship, our flexibility or inflexibility, our acceptance or rejection of people, our ministries, our plans, our programs, our relationships, our grace, our attitudes, our priorities, our openness or closedness, and our growth or lack of growth.

Jesus broke with precious traditions when He ate with tax-gatherers and sinners. And He was criticized for it (Matthew

101

9:11). He broke long and precious traditions when He did not keep His disciples in the fasting tradition (Matthew 9:14). He really offended people when He permitted His hungry disciples to pick grain on the Sabbath and when He himself healed a man on the Sabbath (Matthew 12:1-14).

How did Jesus justify offending people by not going along with carrying out the traditions that meant so much to them? Jesus justified His fresh, flexible, open, gracious, liberal lifestyle by making the compassion of God and the needs of people His traditions. He put people above tradition. He believed that God had created people, not traditions, in God's image.

He believed that people were eternal, not traditions. He believed that godly traditions should serve people; that people should not be slaves to traditions. He believed that God has compassion for people, not for traditions. He believed that God so loved the world that He gave His Son—not that God so loved traditions that He gave us by-laws. He believed that some traditions had become walls that kept people away from God. He believed that people were worshiping traditions and serving them rather than God. He believed that some people had kept and taught traditions so long that they were confusing traditions with essentials to keep, and were teaching these precepts of men as if they were the commandments of God.

Consequently, Jesus had a lot to say that would unlock the handcuffs of traditions. But I am not sure that the church today is listening very carefully.

When criticized about His flexibility with the Sabbath, Jesus said, "The Sabbath was made for man, and not man for the Sabbath" (Mark 2:27). Can we live with that? How about, "The order of the worship service is made for man. Man is not made for it." If we can live with that, then we can permit beneficial change in the order of worship without getting upset.

When Jesus was criticized for violating traditions in His social contacts, He replied, "It is not those who are healthy who need a physician, but those who are sick. But go and learn what this means. I desire compassion, and not sacrifice, for I did not come to call the righteous, but sinners" (Matthew 9:12, 13). Are we listening carefully? Is it possible that our inflexibility about certain traditions keeps people away? Who is the more sick—the people who are outside of Christ, or those who are inside who refuse to change human traditions that, if changed, might say to outsiders, "We care; you are welcome; and here you can be loved and saved"?

Do you think we have no traditions that keep people at a distance? How about the kind of dress we expect, the length of men's hair, the time of the worship service, the kind of music we insist upon or insist against, or the number of times we expect Christians to be at the church building each week?

Jesus came partly to set us free from the kind of legalism that prevents people from loving other people. "It was for freedom that Christ set us free; therefore keep standing firm and do not be subject again to a yoke of slavery" (Galatians 5:1). *Standing firm,* in this verse, refers to standing firm on the freedom Christ has given us. Stand firm on the stand to be flexible. The Jews had hundreds of traditions that they made binding on people. They would judge others by their adherence or non-adherence to those traditions, and they would take their own spiritual temperatures by how well they were keeping or violating those traditions. When Paul said, "Do not be subject again to a yoke of slavery," he was saying, "Don't replace one set of binding traditions with another. If you do, you have merely changed prison cells, but you are still a prisoner."

If we are not careful, any of us can become experts at establishing our own criteria for judging people and churches. To illustrate that few of us are exempt from doing this, let's take the following test. Assign to each of the following items a *1, 2, 3,* or *4.* A *1* stands for unacceptable to you. Give that number to any item that would upset you so much that you would use your influence to change the situation or not to permit it to continue. A *2* means that you will tolerate the item although you do not prefer it. However, you do realize that the item might be preferred by other people, and you do not believe it violates a command from God. A *3* means this item is acceptable to you, but it can be altered without your being upset. A *4* means that you believe the item is acceptable to you and should not be altered. In fact, you would get upset if anyone tried to change it.

_____ 1. Clapping hands in a worship service.

_____ 2. Using classical music as a prelude.

_____ 3. Raising one's hands to pray.

_____ 4. Keeping one's hands down during prayer.

_____ 5. Having the Communion table located in the center front of the church auditorium.

_____ 6. Allowing men without ties and jackets to serve the Lord's Supper.

_____ 7. Allowing a church leader to ride a motorcycle.

_____ 8. Having a mid-week service.

_____ 9. Maintaining the present order of worship.

_____10. Singing choruses in Sunday morning worship.

_____11. Making announcements during the worship hours.

_____12. A preacher's growing a beard.

_____13. Having a Sunday evening service.

_____14. Dismissing a Sunday-night service on a holiday that is traditionally family oriented, such as a Christmas or the Fourth of July, when it falls on a Sunday.

_____15. Wearing jeans at church services.

_____16. Serving coffee in the Sunday school class.

_____17. Having someone besides the preacher doing baptisms.

_____18. Having a woman baptize someone in the worship service.

_____19. Using a guitar in worship.

_____20. Singing an invitational hymn.

_____21. Maintaining the location of the Lord's Supper in the order of worship.

_____22. Using a particular version of the Bible.

_____23. Having the choir wear robes.

_____24. Having the preacher wear a robe.

_____25. Selling religious records or books in the church building.

_____26. A woman's giving the invocation or benediction.

_____27. Working on Sunday.

_____28. Eating meals in the church building.

_____29. Having a nursery for babies.

_____30. Hugging one another at church services.

_____31. Attending movies.

_____32. Participating in any kind of card playing.

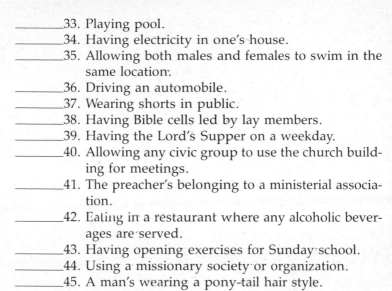

_____33. Playing pool.

_____34. Having electricity in one's house.

_____35. Allowing both males and females to swim in the same location.

_____36. Driving an automobile.

_____37. Wearing shorts in public.

_____38. Having Bible cells led by lay members.

_____39. Having the Lord's Supper on a weekday.

_____40. Allowing any civic group to use the church building for meetings.

_____41. The preacher's belonging to a ministerial association.

_____42. Eating in a restaurant where any alcoholic beverages are served.

_____43. Having opening exercises for Sunday school.

_____44. Using a missionary society or organization.

_____45. A man's wearing a pony-tail hair style.

Every one of the above is on somebody's religious "hit list." Some of us get so uptight about one or more of these that we are willing to throw somebody overboard who wants to change, add, or delete. We'll call a special board meeting, begin a campaign, add some by-laws to the constitution, quit the church, start a new church, or drop friendship with the "offender."

How often we fuss and fight about the non-essentials so fiercely that we elevate them to the status of essentials. Some people live so much to be victorious in keeping their traditions and forcing them onto others that their individual worship does not honor God. In fact, their hearts are far from God and in vain do they worship. They teach traditions of men as if they were the doctrines of God (Matthew 15:7-9).

Jesus made it clear that those Pharisees had become so tied to their traditions and evaluated them so highly that they eventually taught them as being equal in authority to God's commands. Some of those traditions became such big issues that the commands were completely hidden behind them, and so the commands were neglected.

None of us wants to teach our traditions with such authority that people confuse them with the commands of God, but we may do that without realizing it. Here are some ways we do it.

1. We insist that if a certain traditional procedure is changed we will quit the church.
2. We will not be friendly with someone who holds a different opinion about that tradition.
3. We will not permit flexibility in a tradition without raising a verbal fuss.
4. We get up and walk out.
5. We withhold financial support.
6. We make people with differing opinions feel so uncomfortable that they leave the church.

Some people come to worship with real emotional chips on their shoulders. They come armed for battle. They are going to make sure things go their way. They act as Christian Doberman pinscher guard dogs. They watch over the style of music, the version of the Bible, the dress of the participants, and the order of service. When anything gets "out of tradition," they bark and bite. When anyone does that, he has a misplaced heart and an empty, useless worship.

Does that mean that we are given the license to do anything we want to? Of course not. That is a perversion of what real freedom is. Real freedom is not the right to do what we please. If people lived with that kind of freedom, some would drive on the wrong side of the road just to be different.

Real freedom in Christ unshackles us from sin, legalism, traditions, and habits (Romans 6:16; John 8:32, 36). Therefore, we can genuinely quit thinking about ourselves. Then we can serve other people freely. A person who spends a great deal of his time judging others by his own traditions doesn't have either the disposition or the time to care enough about other people to reach out to them in love. Paul was really free to care about people when he could put aside all the ways he had been accustomed to condemning them.

For though I am free from all men, I have made myself a slave to all, that I might win the more.   —1 Corinthians 9:19

For he who was called in the Lord while a slave, is the Lord's freedman; likewise he who was called while free, is Christ's slave.
          —1 Corinthians 7:22

For you were called to freedom, brethren; only do not turn your

freedom into an opportunity for the flesh, but through love serve
one another.   —Galatians 5:13

The Diotrephes-kind of people (3 John 9, 10) gave Paul fits.
They sneaked around to spy out Paul's liberty for the purpose
of putting him and others back into legalistic slavery to traditions (Galatians 2:4). But Paul didn't cave in to that. He in-
sisted that Christians are freed from legalism (Galatians 5:1)
and from seeing God's way through the veil of past traditions
(2 Corinthians 3:15, 16). However, Paul did not permit his
liberty to turn him into an undisciplined man. He remained a
slave—a slave of God to serve people's needs. But he was a
slave who volunteered in response to what God had done for
him. He made himself a slave to others by being flexible.

> And to the Jews I became as a Jew, that I might win Jews; to those
> who are under the Law, as under the Law, though not being
> myself under the Law, that I might win those who are under the
> Law; to those who are without law, as without law, though not
> being without the law of God but under the law of Christ, that I
> might win those who are without law. To the weak I became
> weak, that I might win the weak; I have become all things to all
> men, that I may by all means save some.
>
> 1 Corinthians 9:20-22

It is time that we be willing to dump any traditions that may
have us so crowded that we will not take into our lifeboats the
drowning people around us.

We are not to be standing upon the rock of traditions. Traditions are too often cultural quicksand that we should allow to
change with the time.

God is not trapped inside a Jewish mentality, a Mid-
western mentality, a South Carolina mentality, a Western
mentality, an African mentality, or any other human mentality. He is a big God—bigger than any region and any re-
gional tradition.

The first characteristic we see about God is His creativity.
"In the beginning God created. . . ." He is innovative. Every
person of God who really made a difference in the Bible was
also innovative, creative, and flexible in the non-essentials. To

stifle creativity because we have never done it that way before may be to stop the development of real greatness. Let's allow people the freedom God does.

We are to stand on the rock of Christ. The song writer Edward Mote has captured that truth well.

"On Christ, the solid Rock, I stand;
All other ground is sinking sand."

How many people see us as cold rejectors today? I used to be part of an environment within Christianity that looked at people very critically. Beards were out, mustaches were out, sideburns below the ears were out, hair that touched a man's collar was out, T-shirts without outer shirts were out, wearing jeans to any church function was out, wearing shower clogs in public was out, a person who had gone through a divorce was out, sundresses on a girl were out, a dress less than two inches below the knee was out, shorts were out—and on and on and on the list went.

A person cannot have such a list driven into him for years without some effect on the way he sees people and relates to them. When a brother or sister stood up to speak or sing, the first thing I would do was to go through the check-list to see whether he or she passed the test of acceptability. What a relief to be freed from that! Only as I was freed in Christ did I become more approachable and more willing to approach others with genuine concern about what they really were.

Shooting the Wounded or Healing the Sick?

(Matthew 18:21-35)

Someone has said that the church is the only army that shoots its own wounded. Sometimes, instead of shooting them, we desert them to die on the battlefield all alone. When a fellow Christian falls, he may not fear the wolves on the outside as much as the sheep on the inside who stand ready to trample him to death.

Someone else once asked how many times can a brother or sister goof it before we "shoot him." The person who asked that question was Peter. "Lord how often shall my brother sin against me and I forgive him? Up to seven times?" From Peter's background, he was really being big hearted when he tossed out that "seven" figure, for the Rabbis taught that a person should be forgiven three times but never four. So Peter's count more than doubled expectations. Peter must have thought that his suggestion was a "second miler" suggestion. But Jesus threw the counting game away when He replied, "Seventy times seven." Four hundred and ninety times? You've got to be kidding, Jesus. Who could keep that kind of score? But that was Jesus' point. Have compassion, not a count. Look toward reconciliation, not toward revenge.

One of the beautiful things I notice about little children growing up is their quickness to forget the pains of yesterday and thus be free for both the pleasures of today and progress toward tomorrow.

Our youngest child is in the second grade now. I couldn't count the number of times she has stormed into the house and huffed and puffed up the stairs with the determined commitment that comes out of her mouth, "I'm never going to play with Nicki again. She makes me so mad!" That might happen at 10:45 A.M. By 11:00 A.M., she is ready to die for Nicki, and no one had better try to separate them. I've never seen a little child (we've had four of our own, and there are usually at least ten others around the house) who keeps his accountant pad close at hand, "That's 265 times, just 225 more and then just watch out."

Perhaps that's the reason Matthew introduces the responsibility or forgiveness with Jesus' words, "Truly I say to you, unless you are converted and become like children, you shall not enter the kingdom of heaven" (Matthew 18:3).

We are certainly not to take advantage of the vulnerability and forgiveability of little children, "Whoever causes one of these little ones who believe in Me to stumble, it is better for him that a heavy millstone be hung around his neck, and that he be drowned in the depth of the sea" (Matthew 18:6). But we are to imitate the graciousness of a little child when that child is hurt. Of course, that little child may pout awhile, but before long he is out searching for his playmates. Little children do the "S-R-F" before they are old enough to read about it in Matthew.

Jesus taught us the S-R-F reaction when a brother sins. Search (Matthew 18:12-14), Reprove (Matthew 18:15-20) and Forgive (Matthew 18:21-35).

The first step toward reconciliation is for the person who has been offended to lay his ego aside and to search out the person who has hurt him. Notice who is to take the initiative—the offended person. The sinned against person is not to sit around and say, "It's that other person's fault. If he wants to patch things up, let him take the first step. After all, he caused the problem to begin with; so he should initiate the solution." The goal for searching out is for reconciliation, not for retaliation.

The second step is to reprove (Matthew 18:15-20). The word *reprove* does not mean to chew out, but to reveal the wrong to help the person turn away from it. Exposing frees both the offender and the offended from covering up and from letting the tension fester and build inwardly until something blows. That's another mark of little children. They have the bold honesty to tell their playmates what they did wrong that offended. Now that's getting the cards face up on the table.

The third step Jesus mentioned is to forgive (Matthew 18:21-35). Unless we forgive, we are chained to the past failures and frustrations. Too many people allow the pettiness of the past to erase the potentiality of the present and future.

Have you ever been to a circus or zoo and seen a hugh elephant contained by a tiny, fragile chain and peg? That chain is not strong enough to keep that elephant restricted. Then why does it work? Attendants chained that elephant to a peg when the elephant was a baby. The chain and peg were strong enough then and the elephant became accustomed to being limited by that chain. However, as that elephant grew in size, weight, and strength, he allowed that insignificant chain to continue to control him. The elephant's containment was because of his own self-restrictive decision that had no relationship with the strength of the chain. That elephant was really chained to his past experiences and thus not free to enjoy his present realities.

I wonder how many of us are chained to our past experiences — past alienations from others and past hurts that others have caused us.

To refuse to forgive is to keep our eyes on the negative and not the positive, on the past and not the future, on the hurt and not the healing, on self and not on others.

Some of the greatest accomplishments done for God have come out of ordinary people who did not allow the past actions of others to control their reactions the rest of their lives. Abraham sinned against Sarah, but Sarah refused to allow that to weaken her commitment to her husband; and God blessed her. Moses was angry when the people manufactured a calf and complained against God and Moses, but he freed himself from that and offered to be blotted out of God's book for their sin, and God blessed. Probably no one has been more mistreated by his brothers than was Joseph. However, Joseph named his first son "Making to forget." Joseph did not permit the past sins of others against him to determine his life. Joseph named his second son "Fruitfulness." There is a definite relationship between forgetfulness

111

and fruitfulness. Had Joseph not forgotten about his troubles first, the fruit would have been rotten and destructive.

Jesus illustrated that principle in the reaction of the guy who was forgiven but would not forget a debt owed him. That man was forgiven the equivalent of sixty million days' pay. But that forgiven person went out and allowed a debt of one hundred days' pay owed him to eat him up. So his fruit was bitter. He did not pass on the grace he had received. We love to be forgiven, but to forgive is something *else*. We want people to forget the times and ways we have fumbled the ball, but forgetting when others drop the ball on us is another matter. The more seriously we sin against another, the more eager we are for them to forgive. But then we can easily turn around and carry grudges over the smallest things done against us.

To refuse to forgive acknowledges many things: (1) We are not developing the beatitudes that can keep us buoyed up—humble, sensitive to others, self controlled, merciful, and the rest. (2) We think we deserve to be forgiven, but others do not. (3) We think we are more important than God. He forgives, but our sense of self-importance will not. (4) We deny that God can work all things out for good; so we take control. (5) We forget that everyone sins, and that includes us. (6) We really do not appreciate God's forgiveness and, thus, forfeit it (Matthew 18:35). (7) We fail to empathize with others. (8) We do not think that it is worth our living for what Jesus died for—forgiveness of people.

That man who did not forgive the comparatively small debt against him had evidently forgotten the hurt he had gone through before his forgiveness. He had evidently forgotten that he was ready to throw in the towel until he was forgiven. He had probably forgotten he had no future, no hope, and no peace without the forgiveness of another.

Jesus taught his disciples to practice limitless forgiveness in two ways. (1) The quantity of the sins—no amount is too many times—"seventy times seven." (2) The quality of the sin—no category of sin is so bad that we should withhold forgiveness. Jesus elsewhere taught that any sin and blasphemy shall be forgiven except blasphemy against the Spirit; so He expects us to forgive any category of sin committed against us.

Forgiving others has several built-in benefits to oneself.

(1) *Forgiveness affects our emotional health.* Carrying grudges pours emotional negative feelings into our inner system. The person who will not forgive others spends a lot of energy justifying himself for his own negative activities. He takes the position that he is always right. The person who always has to be right is in for unhappiness, not joy.

(2) *Forgiveness enhances friendship and fellowship.* The perfectionist who cannot forgive lives a lonely life.

(3) *Forgiveness affects physical health.* We are discovering that there are significant therapeutic values in belonging to others. A nine-year study of 7000 people in Alameda County, California, revealed that people with few ties to others had two to five times the death rate of those who had more ties (*Friends Can Be Good Medicine*, California Department of Mental Health, 1981). That study showed that connection with others was more important to maintaining health than smoking, drinking, exercise, or diet. Forgiveness is a bridge that keeps people connected to each other. Doctors Carl and Stephanie Simonton, who work with cancer patients, have done substantial research that points to the theory that people who have a great tendency to hold resentment and a marked inability to forgive are more cancer-prone than those who forgive (Bruce Larson, *There's a Lot More to Health Than Not Being Sick,* Word, 1981). Research from many different areas reveals that a poor mental disposition is a key prediction of physical deterioration. Dr. George Valliant of Cambridge Hospital in Cambridge, Massachusetts, concludes that a person's mental health determines his physical well-being more than whether or not he smokes, drinks, is overweight, or has parents who died at an early age. Valliant states that people who are better at loving other people and who have satisfying personal relations avoid early aging while their counterparts start deteriorating during middle age (Larson, *There's a Lot More to Health . . .*) .

(4) *Forgiveness affects our spiritual health.* Jesus said that God will not forgive us if we do not forgive others.

"For if you forgive men for their transgressions, your heavenly Father will also forgive you. But if you do not forgive men, then your Father will not forgive your transgressions" (Matthew 6:14-15).

"So shall My heavenly Father also do to you, if each of you does not forgive his brother from your heart: (Matthew 18:35).

No wonder God wants us to make forgiveness a life-style characteristic. It affects our inner lives, our social lives, our physical lives, and our spiritual lives. Nothing goes untouched when we forgive or refuse to forgive.

What hinders us from forgiving others? Here are a few factors:
1. Placing blame to reduce the pain.
2. Thinking that to say, "I forgive," equals forgiveness.
3. Thinking that denial of being hurt is forgiveness.
4. Thinking that avoiding the person will keep the relationship corrected.
5. Thinking that if the person does some kind of compensating act that he doesn't need your forgiveness.

There are several aspects—actions one needs to perform—that are poured into real forgiveness:
1. See the other person as a person of worth.
2. Think positive thoughts about the other person. Make his good actions take priority in your thinking rather than his bad actions.
3. Let go of the past. Unless a person lets go of the past problems, failures, and actions, he does not forgive. That calls for an inner commitment to let go, but some people want time only to do that without their willful commitment.
4. Let go of self defenses, demands, and disgusts.
5. Release the animosity that you held against the other.
6. Trust the other person again. It is a farce to say, "I forgive you, but I'll never trust you again." Who wants that kind of forgiveness?
7. Forgive even if the other person does not repent. That can motivate repentance.
8. Reach out with acts that show you really care about the other person.
9. Restore closeness with the other person. One goal of

forgiveness is to reaffirm love and reconstruct the relationship.

Forgiveness has not really happened if two people say, "I forgive," but continue to withdraw from each other, refuse to talk, go their own way, and ignore and neglect one another. There is not real forgiveness if we purposely keep the other person out of our world who was at one time in it. Forgiveness is absent when a person judges the actions of another person by the past hurts. Instead of forgiveness, which releases us from the past, there is a fettering, which chains us to the past.

When one person continues to evaluate another by past hurts, it causes that other person to be very uncomfortable, for he realizes his motives are already determined by the other person. That does not allow room for changes, but only for chains. To keep yourself or another person chained to the past is a terrible and lonely way to live.

We hold to the past with resentment, and we look to the future with suspicion. Therefore, we cannot enjoy the only time we have—now. We cannot change the past, and we cannot control the future; so why try either?

Little children who have been emotionally or physically hurt by a playmate know the secret. They forgive quickly so they can get on with enjoying the next games with people they have come to love and need. And unless we become as little children, we will not enter the kingdom of Heaven—nor enjoy life on earth. Forgiveness is the key that locks up the past but unlocks the future and frees us from both—to live life now and to live it more abundantly.

Forgive and be free. Release the elephant. Don't let the littleness of past hurts become links of a chain that binds you to a weak peg. We are all bigger than that—even little children.

Is He Going Under?

(Matthew 26:36–27:54)

Jesus had been rejected by nearly everyone at one point or another in His life. His hometown people had turned their backs on Him; multitudes of His followers had walked away from Him; His mother had tried to take Him back home; His half-brothers had not believed in Him. Before that dreadful night was over, all of His apostles would also flee from Him. Only One had not forsaken Him—His Heavenly Father. But that, too, was soon to happen; and Jesus knew it.

The Garden

Jesus knew that He was to die for the sins of all mankind. He had foretold that several times (Matthew 16:21-23; 17:9, 12; 20:28). He had approached Jerusalem knowing what was going to happen. He had told the disciples about it very plainly, as we see in Luke 18:31-33.

> And He took the twelve aside and said to them, "Behold, we are going up to Jerusalem, and all things which are written through the prophets about the Son of Man will be accomplished. For He will be delivered up to the Gentiles, and will be mocked and mistreated and spit upon, and after they have scourged Him, they will kill Him; and the third day He will rise again."

But when the time of torture and death drew near, Jesus asked God to detour the plan: "My Father, if it is possible, let this cup pass from Me" (Matthew 26:39). Why would Jesus want to bypass what He had predicted—indeed, what He had come to earth to do? With what was He wrestling in the garden?

Physical death is bad enough, especially death with all the torture of crucifixion. No man could face it without shrinking. But for Jesus there was more. There was the weight of sins not His own. There was the whole load of man's guilt. To take the place of sinful humanity, Jesus must suffer all that sinners suffer. He must be cut off from God—spiritual death.

He would accept the wages of sin himself; He would voluntarily take our sins as His own. The prophets foretold that this would happen: "But He was pierced through for our transgressions, He was crushed for our iniquities; the chastening for our well-being fell upon Him" (Isaiah 53:5).

Worse than physical death was that separation. He had never been separated from God, even for a split second. He was God (John 1:1). But He would be separated from God for the benefit of mankind.

Jesus prayed three times for such a cup to pass, but He did not give in to His feelings or His grief (Matthew 26:39). He knew that He would have to fulfill His commitment. So He handed His feelings over to God and asked that God's will be done.

I wonder how many of us could have done that? It is easy for us to rationalize and say that what we want to do is God's will. We get these feelings and think God has spoken to us. But how many times was that voice the voice of our inner selves rather than the voice of God? Confusing God's will with our selfish desires or feelings is a common fault of us humans. Since we can't become God, we try to whittle Him down to our size.

If Jesus had succumbed to His feelings that night in the garden, He would never have gone to the cross. How many crosses have we passed up because our feelings said no? We must follow Jesus' example and make decisions based upon commitments rather than feelings. Instead of following His feelings, which said no, Jesus followed His commitment, which said go. That is why He did not resist when the mob with their swords and clubs came to take Him away (Matthew 26:47, 50).

The Trial

It would have been nice if one person had stood up at Jesus' hearing to say a good word in appreciation of all that Jesus

117

had done in the three years of His ministry, but no one did. Although no one said anything good about Him, it was still hard to find anyone to say something bad about Him. Pilate pressed for some kind of charge against Jesus: "What accusation do you bring against this man?" (John 18:29). But all they could say was something like "We would not have brought Him to you if He were not bad." (See John 18:30.)

Pilate saw through their facade and told them to take Jesus and judge Him for themselves (John 18:31). So the Jews drummed up a political charge, thinking that Pilate would pay attention to them then. But saying that Jesus was a revolutionary (Luke 23:2) did not impress Pilate either: "I find no guilt in this man" (Luke 23:4). Then the Jews finally spit out what was really bothering them: "He stirs up the people" (Luke 23:5).

The hypocrisy of the religious elite was made crystal clear during the trial of Jesus. After they turned Jesus over to the Romans, they would not enter into the Roman building "in order that they might not be defiled, but might eat the Passover" (John 18:28). So Pilate had to go in and out of the building; he would go in to talk to Jesus, and then come out again to talk with the Jews (John 18:29, 33, 38; 19:4, 9, 13).

What a sad perversion of religion! These religious men did not want to touch Gentile property that would make them religiously unclean and keep them from partaking of the Passover. They took much pains to keep their outsides clean, but their insides were filled with schemes of murder.

In order to get rid of Jesus, His enemies lied, blasphemed, and murdered. Yet they would enter into their religious observances, pretending that they were "holy" people and that all was well between them and God.

Do we ever act that way? Do we ever disregard the mistreatment of a fellow man and at the same time maintain perfect attendance at our rituals? Do we ever spread false gossip about someone during the week and then praise God with the same mouths on Sunday? Are we peacemakers while worshiping, but soon afterwards become destroyers of the peace by being unkind, critical, or demanding? We may say we would never have treated Jesus so terribly, but we must remember that how we treat others is how we are treating Him (Matthew 25:31-40).

Pilate declared that Jesus had no guilt; so he tried to maneuver His release. It was customary to release one prisoner of the Jews' choice at the Passover feast. Pilate gave them a choice between the mild, compassionate Jesus and Barabbas, a notorious robber, murderer, and insurrectionist (Matthew 27:16; Luke 23:19; John 18:40). Pilate must have thought they would choose Jesus, but Pilate had misjudged how deeply hatred could run and how violent the envious could become.

The "religious" people chose to release Barabbas over Jesus—the sinner over the saint, the man over God-in-flesh, the thief over the truth, the crook over the Christ. And the chief priests and elders persuaded the lay people (the multitudes) to ask for Barabbas' release and for Jesus' death.

Pilate could hardly believe the choice they had made. Even though he was a pagan, he knew it was terribly unjust to kill an innocent man. So he tried another approach. If they saw this man tortured, he thought, their thirst for blood and revenge would be satisfied, and they would allow Jesus to be freed. He had Jesus whip-lashed severely (John 19:1). The soldiers mocked Him and put thorns upon His brow. Pilate then brought Jesus out for the people to see, hoping their hearts would melt. He said, "Behold, the man" (John 19:5).

Instead of crying out for clemency, the people cried out for His crucifixion. Pilate was reluctant; he could find no fault in Jesus. He made further efforts to have Him released (John 19:12), but the Jews threatened him: "If you release this Man, you are no friend of Caesar; everyone who makes himself out to be a king opposes Caesar (John 19:12).

History tells us that Pilate had been on shaky ground with Caesar before. He knew he was walking on thin ice in his relationship with the emperor. His political career might be finished if a group of Jewish leaders would go to Rome and report that Pilate was tolerating a rebel who claimed to be a king. To save himself, Pilate ordered Jesus crucified.

Before we are too hard on Pilate, we must search our own practices. Do we sometimes allow the crowd around us to weaken our convictions about Jesus? Do we turn away from Jesus in order to save our own faces? We want to be liked and accepted so much that we may not stand up for Jesus in certain issues at home, at school, or at work. Pilate's attitude lives on even today.

The Cross

The captain of the guard wondered what kind of man that was on the center cross. Crucifixion was not new to the captain, but never had he crucified a man like that. Other men had to be tied to the cross while it lay on the ground in order to keep them there while the nails were driven into their hands. They would scream, curse, struggle, or weep; but not the man in the middle. He lay on the cross, giving no resistance. He remained still while the nails penetrated His skin and the blood gushed out.

Crucifixion was the most disgraceful and cruel way to die. It was nine o'clock in the morning when Jesus was nailed to the cross. Yet in the midst of His pain and agony, He thought of others: "Father, forgive them; for they do not know what they are doing" (Luke 23:34). He looked down upon the crowd and saw His mother. He knew how devastated she must have been and He asked one of His disciples to look after her (John 19: 26, 27).

Every breath Jesus took on the cross was accompanied by suffering—thirst, fever, dizziness, throbbing, swelling, burning. The experience was so inhumane that Roman law would not permit a Roman citizen to be crucified. Even the brutal executioners allowed a special drink to deaden the pain. Jesus refused the pain-killer, but later allowed a moistened sponge to be put on His parched lips (Matthew 27:34, 48).

As Jesus breathed his last, He cried out, "My God My God, why hast Thou forsaken Me?" (Matthew 27:46). Jesus then uttered, "It is finished" (John 19:30). Was Jesus sinking for good? Was walking on the water over for Jesus?

I once saw a poster that pictured a stream that was winding back and forth through a meadow. With each turn, the stream got narrower and narrower until it finally made a bend and ended—so it seemed. But several yards beyond the "end" of the stream was a beautiful lake with the moon shining upon it. The words on the poster said, "What appears to be the end may really be just a new beginning."

What was ahead after the cross? A new beginning.

Check Your COMMITMENT
Studies from Matthew

13

by Knofel Staton

He Is Walking on Water Again

(Matthew 28)

It was not fantasy. It was not an illusion. It was not an assumption. It was not just a hunch. It was real. Jesus was dead.

Not one of His close disciples expected to see Him alive again. So they did not believe the report that Jesus was alive (Matthew 28:8-10). In fact, words about His still being alive "appeared to them as nonsense, and they would not believe them" (Luke 24:11). Even after they saw Him, they thought they were seeing just His Spirit (Luke 24:37).

The evidence for the resurrection is beyond logical disputing. Here are some of those evidences.

The Evidence of the Resurrection

What evidence kept the first-century people from denying the resurrection?

The life of Jesus. Unless we could prove Jesus was alive in the first place, we wouldn't have much chance at proving a resurrection. But Jesus was highly visible. He was not an underground figure. Outside the New Testament account, other sources affirm Jesus' earthly life: Josephus, Tacitus Pliny, Suetonius, Andrian, Antonius, Lucian, Celsus, Julian, and other historians of the time.

The credibility of the New Testament account. There were many witnesses in the first century who could have challenged any errors written in the New Testament. The New Testament is not just what the church wanted us to believe, but the facts to be believed because of the evidence.

The reality of Jesus' death. Unless it can be affirmed that Jesus really died, we cannot affirm a resurrection. But the facts surrounding His death leave absolutely no doubt that it was real. He did not just faint. He underwent a scourging that, according to Eusebius, left a man's veins, muscles, and bowels exposed. Weakened after a sleepless, foodless night and that beating, He was nailed to a cross where He hung for six hours.

His enemies knew He was dead. They came to watch Him die, and they were not about to leave without being satisfied. A spear was thrust into His side for the express purpose of being absolutely sure. The disciples knew He was dead. The centurion, an expert on executions, knew He was dead (Mark 15:44, 45). Joseph of Arimathea knew He was dead (John 19:38); he would hardly be interested in providing a tomb for a live man.

Yes, they did indeed bury a dead man. In fact, they buried Him in such a way that He would stay buried forever. They wrapped Him up like a mummy along with a hundred pounds of spices. Try getting out of that!

The conduct of the disciples. Before the resurrection, everyone of them deserted Jesus. Peter wouldn't admit that he knew Jesus, not even to an insignificant maiden (Matthew 26:69-75). But after the resurrection, he replied boldly to the most powerful group of men in Palestine when they ordered him to quit speaking about Jesus' death and resurrection: "We cannot stop speaking what we have seen and heard" (Acts 4:20). Every one of the apostles (except Judas) followed Peter's example. It is thought that each one was executed for his proclamation (except John, who was exiled on a rugged island and later died a natural death). Without the reality of the resurrection, it is highly unlikely that these men would have stuck it out as they did.

Some say the apostles wanted to believe Jesus had risen, and so they convinced themselves that he had. No, not one of them believed Jesus would rise again. They didn't believe He had risen when the women told them He had. In fact, they were reluctant to believe it even when Jesus appeared to them.

The historical changes. Look at the calendar. It is dated from the time of Jesus. People would not have changed their calendars on the basis of hoax.

Consider the existence of the church. It gathered its members from those same people who had said to Pilate, "Crucify Him." Many who became part of the church would be kicked out of the synagogue, disowned by their families, and discharged from their jobs; yet the church grew by leaps and bounds. People who had formerly hated each other joined in loving fellowship. The power of the resurrection broke down many barriers.

Consider the church ordinances. They point to a literal resurrection. Immersion reflects the death, burial, and resurrection of Jesus and our own new life (Romans 6). The Lord's Supper emphasizes Jesus' death, but also the future and Jesus' return.

Even the day of worship changed. After the resurrection, Christians worshiped on the first day of the week instead of the seventh. The Jews would have utterly rejected such a change except for the fact that Jesus arose on the first day of the week. The gathering was a weekly celebration that Jesus was alive.

Those who never questioned the resurrection. Jesus' enemies did not challenge the resurrection. The chief priests paid the soldiers to lie and say that the disciples stole the body, but they knew He had risen. King Agrippa, Pilate, Felix, and Festus heard about the resurrection and did not challenge it. Many priests believed and became Christians (Acts 6:7).

Even the pagan philosophers in Athens did not all deny the resurrection. Some of them mocked, but some of them became Christians (Acts 17:18-34).

Many Jews around the world knew about the resurrection. Jesus arose during a major Jewish festival, when Jerusalem was crowded with Jews from every corner of the world. Many of them told of the resurrection when they returned home. When Paul preached in the various cities, none of the Jews denied its reality. Many rejected Paul's teaching about the temple and the law, but it is not recorded that they denied his report of the resurrection.

It is interesting to note that the denials of the resurrection come mainly from the philosophers and theologians of the modern era who do not believe that God created the world or is in charge today. It becomes logical to deny the resurrection if we have no belief in supernatural powers behind the world and our lives on it. But it is not logical to deny the resurrection on historical grounds.

The Conversion of Paul. Paul heard about the resurrection, but he did not believe it at first. When the risen Jesus appeared to him, Paul knew. Then he considered all of the learning and knowledge he had gained up to that time to be rubbish (Philippians 3:4-14). He faced death many times, but he was absolutely convinced that death for him would be gain because Jesus had risen. Such a devoted Jew and ardent persecutor of Christians could not be so drastically changed on the basis of a hoax.

Jesus' actual appearances. For forty days, Jesus appeared to people in His bodily form. We don't know exactly how many people saw Him or where they saw Him. We do know about one crowd of five hundred men (1 Corinthians 15:6). Following is a list of His known appearances:

Mary Magdalene—John 20:14-18; Mark 16:9
Other Women—Matthew 28:1, 9, 10
Simon Peter—Luke 24:34; 1 Corinthians 15:5
Two men on a road—Mark 16:12; Luke 24:13-33
The apostles except Thomas—Mark 16:14; Luke 24:36-43; John 20:19-25
The apostles with Thomas—John 20:26-29
Seven by the Lake of Tiberias—John 21:1-23
More than five hundred—1 Corinthians 15:6
James—1 Corinthians 15:7
The eleven—Matthew 28:16-20; 1 Corinthians 15:7
At the ascension—Mark 16:19; Luke 24:50, 51; Acts 1:3-12
Stephen—Acts 7:55, 56
Paul—Acts 9:3-6; 1 Corinthians 15:8
Paul in the temple—Acts 22:17-21
Paul in prison—Acts 23:11
John on Patmos—Revelation 1:9-19

The Good News

Confucius' tomb is not empty. Buddha's tomb is not empty. Mohammed's tomb is not empty. Joseph Smith's tomb is not empty. Jim Jones' tomb is not empty. Mr. Moon's tomb will not be empty.

But Jesus' tomb is empty! He has risen! It is no wonder the early Christians could not greet each other with a simple "hello." They had to express the joy they felt in their hearts. The greeted each other saying, "He is risen!" And the response, "He is risen indeed!"

After His resurrection, Jesus shared three vital truths with His apostles:

1. *His power.* "All authority has been given to Me in heaven and on earth" (Matthew 28:18). Jesus is indeed Lord of Lords and King of Kings. When He came to earth, He emptied himself of deity and put on humanity (Philippians 2:6, 7). In the resurrection, He emptied himself of humanness and resumed deity. Consequently, nothing is impossible with Him.

2. *Our purpose,* "Go therefore and make disciples of all the nations, baptizing them in the name of the Father and the Son and the Holy Spirit, teaching them to observe all that I commanded you" (Matthew 28:19, 20). Jesus' followers are not to be in a ministry of maintenance—just keeping the status quo. We are to be in a ministry of growth. And it isn't to be a multiplication of sameness, but of diversity. We are to evangelize all peoples—all categories, all groupings, all languages, all ethnics.

It is easy to forget the purpose of the church. We can get so busy doing so many good things that we neglect the one most important thing—to evangelize. We live in a lost world. Today, over three billion people do not know Jesus Christ. If they stood in a line shoulder to shoulder, and we drove by that line at fifty miles per hour twelve hours a day, it would take us nearly three and one half years to get to the end of the line. And then that line would be 26,607 miles longer. Those are people God loves and for whom Jesus died. They are people about whom Jesus thought when He said, "No one comes to the Father, but through Me" (John 14:6).

This is not the concern, priority, or task of the government. It is not the concern, priority, or task of AT&T, G.M., Boeing, or any other industry or business. It is not the concern, priority, or task of the University of California or any other public college or university. God has given this concern, priority, and task to the church.

During this year, the line of non-Christians will get 7,665 miles longer. It will outgrow the Christian line by three times if we continue to keep the same level of concern, priority, and action of our past.

3. *His presence.* "And lo, I am with you always, even to the end of the age." What does it mean for Jesus to say, "I am with you always?"

It means God is with us. No wonder we read that Christians have become the dwelling place of God (Ephesians 2:22).

It means power is with us. The God who said, "Let there be light," and light appeared, is a big, big God! And God in all of His bigness is with us. He deserves a standing ovation just to be willing to be with little nobodies. When power and bigness are with us, possibility is with us! Some of us have talked down possibility thinking so much that we live out impossibility thinking. No wonder we don't grow much. We've forgotten who is with us. So we think it's impossible to go to all peoples—the hungry, the thirsty, the lost.

It means love is with us. God is love. And His love lives inside us so He can love others through us. No one will ever come to faith in God who has not experienced the love of God. And it is not enough to say, "I love you, but I don't have to like you." What a cop-out from involvement! Can you hear God saying to us, "I love you, but I sure don't like you"? In Romans 12:10, we read, "Be devoted to one another." Do you know the Greek word there is the Greek word for friendship love. The reason it is translated, "Be devoted," is that's what friends do. They stick with each other. I've heard it said all of my life, "God can command our minds but not our emotions; so I don't have to like you." I've got news for you—God created my emotions, and He's the master of my emotions, and He *can* command my emotions. And He tells me to be friends with one another. God is love. If God is with us, then friendship is also with us. Jesus was and is our friend. We need to be friends with each other. People need friends, not just people.

It means forgiveness is with us. We can forgive because the divine Forgiver lives in us. Could it be that one of the reasons many people do not become Christians is because they do not see us forgiving one another very much?

Whom is Jesus with? *You!* Believe it! Put your name on it. You may say, "But I've goofed!" He replies, "I know that, and I am still with you."

How long will He be with us? Forever! In good times, in bad times; when you're well and when you're sick; when you're on the mountain tops and when you're down in the valleys. When you get down into the valleys of gloom and the shadows of darkness, guess who's beat you there. "Even though I walk through the valley of the shadow of death, I fear no evil; for Thou art with me" (Psalm 23:4).

Indeed, we, too, can walk through the waters because He is with us.

When you pass through the waters, I will be with you; and through the rivers, they will not overflow you. When you walk through the fire, you will not be scorched, nor will the flame burn you (Isaiah 43:2).

Thus says the Lord, who makes a way through the sea and a path through the mighty waters ... "Do not call to mind the former things, Or ponder things of the past. Behold, I will do something new, now it will spring forth; will you not be aware of it? I will even make a roadway in the wilderness, rivers in the desert" (Isaiah 43:16, 18, 19).

The storm may be raging and the waves may be rugged, but He has already risen. And He is with you. Therefore, with Him—you, too, can walk on the water.

CHECK THESE BOOKS
by Knofel Staton

God's Plan for Church Leadership. What is God's plan for leadership? Where can you find role models for God's brand of leadership? Staton gives practical, Biblical help in answering these questions to strike the balance God demands.

Discovering My Gifts for Service. A useful workbook designed for both individual and group study. This workbook will help any Christian determine his God-given abilities and maximize his service in the church.

Check Your Discipleship. A penetrating look at the lives of Jesus and His disciples, with practical application to make our own lives like theirs.

Check Your Homelife. A practical guide to make life around your house more peaceful, more loving, and more Christ-like.

Check Your Morality. A helpful look at such issues as abortion, homosexuality, pornography, alcohol, and more. Staton offers fresh insight from a Biblical perspective.

Available at your Christian bookstore or

STANDARD
PUBLISHING